A
Simply
Homemade
Clean

A
Simply
Homemade
Clean

Lisa Barthuly

Healthy Life Press
Orlando, Florida

A SIMPLY HOMEMADE CLEAN

www.HomesteadOriginals.com
©2012, 2013 Lisa Barthuly All Rights Reserved.

Published by:

Healthy Life Press – 2603 Drake Drive – Orlando, FL 32810
www.healthylifepress.com

Cover Image: © Sandra Cunningham | Dreamstime.com
For internal photo credits, see page v.
Cover and Internal Design: Judy Johnson
Edited by: Melonie Kennedy www.AmericanVirtueMagazine.com

Printed in the United States of America

Library of Congress Cataloging-in-Publication Data
Barthuly, Lisa
  A Simply Homemade Clean

ISBN 978-1-9392-6708-5
1. Natural Cleaners; 2. Homesteading - Natural Cleaners

DEDICATION

Adonai, you turned this heart toward home – there aren't words enough to thank you.

Yeshua Ha Mashiach you gave all . . . for me . . . I love you and your Torah.

To my beloved and my children, you are my daily inspiration and I love you!

Table of Measurements/Abbreviations Used:

C is one cup (8 oz of liquid)

Cs is plural for cups

Dropper: one "dropper" full is 10 drops from the
dropper of a 1 oz essential oil bottle

1 oz is one fluid ounce (oz is also plural for ounces)

1 Q is one quart

1 tsp is one teaspoon (tsp is also plural for teaspoons)

TB (TBs) TB is one tablespoon; TBs is plural

The following stock photos are used with permission:

CONTENTS

A Homemade Clean

Somewhere along the way, it seems we lost our gumption; the desire to make things ourselves. Gone are the days of God's ways, and using what He gave us. We've changed our mindset and not for the better.

We've bound ourselves to the man-made, and to ultra consumerism. There are a slew of retailers just waiting for us with anything and everything we could need; packaged up all pretty, with no thought or effort required. It is the manifestation of 'progress' . . . right?

I don't 'buy' that.

I've found that we are being led like sheep to the slaughter in so many areas of our 'modern', 'convenient' lives; most certainly in the area of "clean"– be it our homes or our bodies.

We have stores on every corner, we can flip open our laptops and have just about anything delivered right to our doors. We are an 'on demand' society. We have no patience and we want things the easy way. Has there ever been a time in man's history with so modern medical 'miracles' and advances . . . yet SO many cancers, illnesses and horrible diseases?

In a nutshell, we're killing ourselves, folks.

Let's be honest, it IS easier to toss a bottle of Pine Cleaner and chemical laden body lotion in our shopping cart at the store than make it up at home. It does take more effort on our part to make things ourselves. However, we are all too happy to fill our homes with every man made toxin ever created — in fact, we whine "we MUST have them, we deserve them — we work HARD, they make our lives easier — we're soooo busy!"

The truth is, the 'almighty dollar' of the companies producing these toxic products and our selfish nature has trumped anything else in life . . . we're even sacrificing our children to it.

"Not so!" you say? Think again.

Why, when we know that formaldehyde, arsenic, phosphates, naphthalene, parabens and so many more of these toxins and chemicals are in the products we use every day; are we bringing them into our homes and using them on our bodies . . . on our children?

If we knew how to change this and make our own cleaning products to replace the toxic, commercial ones…would we? Would we put forth the effort required?

The desire to make my own products stemmed from the frugal, self reliant side of me. I wanted simple; homemade; natural. Remember the definition of simple is NOT 'easier.' Living "simply" in our times, means making a deliberate choice to differ from the mainstream of today's societal norm.

My desire changed over to sheer determination, when one of my children was diagnosed with a myriad of allergies, chemical sensitivities, and asthma. After much study and research, we were determined that we could not have those products in our home, they are useless (when God has provided all we need to make our own) and harmful to everyone in our home.

Join me, as I show you how to easily make your own natural, homemade, handcrafted products that are not only less expensive but truly better for our families, our home and God's Creation.

Homemade Cleaners for the Home

W e've been hoodwinked. We have been led to believe we must have every cleaner on the market – one for each room, appliance, and item in our home. Not so. You can feasibly make just a few homemade products, with just a few ingredients, that will do the bulk of your cleaning.

We can make our own cleaners that do the job and cost so much less; it just takes a little effort and a little desire on our part. This effort and desire reaps benefits for us, our whole family and our Heavenly Father's Creation.

I'll spare you all the studies and stats of how potentially terrible commercial cleaners are for us, our children, and our environment. (You can easily find tons of this information on the Internet.) They can cause a myriad of cancers; liver dysfunction; a host of lung and other diseases; they can contribute to the massive influx of ADD/ADHD, asthma, reproductive issues, and all the allergies we now have. Notice how we've even chemically anti-bacterialized ourselves to death; believe it or not some bacteria ARE good for us.

One fact I find extremely interesting is courtesy of the Toronto Indoor Air Commission Study (okay, I'll quote ONE study). Did you know the homekeeper is approximately 55 percent more likely to develop cancers, over those women working outside the home? Why? We're exposing ourselves day in and day out (and our families) to all these toxins. We LIVE in them, breathe them, bathe in them; everything we touch has been cleaned by some toxic carcinogen and all of these seep into our systems through our skin, lungs, foods and water.

Much of what is housed in our local store's cleaning aisle is just plain overpriced, unhealthy and flat out unnecessary.

Grab yourself a box or three of some good ol' fashioned 20 Mule Team Borax®, then take a left and head to the baking aisle. Huh? Yes, the baking aisle. Grab yourself a few gallons of white vinegar and a few bags of baking soda and you're on your way to making your own cleaners!

Homemade Cleaners Starter Kit

To get going on making your own homemade cleaners, gather your ingredients in one safe spot. This not only keeps you organized, but keeps your supplies together, thus making it simple when it comes time to make up what you need and confining them in a place where no one can mistakenly get into them. Be sure to mark all of your containers, spray bottles, etc., with your permanent marker, clearly stating the contents. I'll even note my recipe on the bottle or label.

(REMINDER: Although these items are natural ingredients, they still need to be treated with caution just like any toxic cleaner. Keep them all away from children and never mix vinegar and bleach.
Also remember that some people have allergies, so always test a small area before going all out.)

Here is a shopping list to get you going down the path to making your own natural homemade cleaners. Many of these items are probably in your home right now.

Homemade Cleaners Starter Kit List

Baking Soda
White Vinegar
Apple Cider Vinegar
Borax
Olive Oil

Lavender Essential Oil
Tea Tree Essential Oil
Eucalyptus Essential Oil
Grapefruit Seed Extract
Orange Essential Oil (or any citrus essential you love)

Empty Sprayer Bottles
Old Washcloths and Rags
Old Toothbrush
Green Scrubbie Pads
Old Glass Canning Jars and Old Plastic Containers (reuse those sour cream or cottage cheese containers.)
Permanent Marker

Now, you can start out with just ONE of the above listed essential oils. If I had to pick just one, I'd go with lavender or tea tree for cleaning. All of the oils listed above have natural antibacterial properties and take very small amounts to do the job. These frugal, natural cleaners you make up yourself will cost pennies on the dollar versus their commercial counterparts.

Essential Oils

Essential oils add powerful properties to our homemade creations and are so versatile; whether it's toilet powder or sugar scrub, window cleaner or lotion bars. Essential oils offer up not only beautiful, truly natural fragrances; but antibacterial, antiviral, and antifungal properties. However, did you know of essential oils role in healing and rebuilding our bodies?

Essential oils are the heart of herbs, plants and trees; God's gifts to us for His way of healing and caring for these bodies He created. Dating back to biblical times, oils were used for anointing and healing the sick. Scientific clinical research studies of today even confirm and reveal that many oils contain very high levels of stimulating immune system properties and a host of healthy benefits for us.

Essential oils are small in molecular structure, therefore have the ability of permeating the skin and entering the bloodstream, and from there entering our cell structure. Using them in our homes and making them a part of our everyday lives is a great blessing to us. Breathing them in, using them in our laundry that therefore touches our skin, in our linen sprays, cleaners, aroma therapies, in our home-made lotions and salves . . . is only wise; they get rid of the bad and give us the good.

Did you know that just a drop of cassia essential oil in water makes a great mouth gargle that not only kills germs but is a decay preventative? A few drops of lemon essential oil in a pint of witch hazel makes a wonderful skin toner for pennies. Frankincense is an amazing germ killer and disinfectant, but also rebuilds and renews our cells. Frankincense also supports our immune system, increases our leukocyte activity to defend the body against infections, is an anti-tumoral, anti-inflammatory . . . and SO much more. What about hyssop? It is revered for its respiratory system support, not to mention its recorded ability to help heal a host of diseases and ailments. Mix a couple drops of lavender essential oil with a teaspoon of olive oil and rub on the temples for headache relief.

The list of uses for essential oils is endless. I use numerous essential oils in my home, our cleaners, homemade remedies, my handcrafted creations, and in our prayer life; they are truly amazing!

Vinegar & Baking Soda:
The Building Blocks

Years ago, when I really started looking at labels and researching just WHAT was in some of the products I was bringing into my home and using on my family. I was shocked that this stuff was even ALLOWED on the store shelf to be purchased by (trusting) consumers in the first place. I started weeding these products OUT of our lives, and learning how to make my own with natural, real ingredients. The skin is our biggest organ and everything you put on it or around it gets absorbed INTO it.

I knew I needed to make changes, NOW.

I started out with what I call the 'building blocks' of natural cleaning; baking soda and vinegar. They are two very simple, natural products that are inexpensive and were easy to start my 'clean routine' with. With just these two items, as a foundation, I can keep a sparkling homestead. I already keep these items on hand for multiple uses around our homestead, and really… can you get any cheaper or more natural products for cleaning your home?

Vinegar and baking soda are a frugal solution to the expensive fancy specialty 'cleaners' that you'll find lining aisles of shelf space at your local grocery store. (That their million dollar ad campaigns say you 'just have to have.') If it has skull and crossbones on the label, I do not want that product in my home. I don't want that stuff around my children, nor do I want to pay the outrageous price they fetch, either.

Vinegar and baking soda are easily found in large bulk packages (in the FOOD aisles), are easily stored, and I stock them for a variety of uses around our homestead – keeping our home clean is just one of them. Stocking these items in bulk as I do, I am not going to 'run out' of any of my homemade cleaning products and have to run to the grocery store. In fact, since these items are 'foods,' chances are good that you will find them in bulk through your co-op or at Costco for a great price.

Using vinegar and baking soda as the foundation of the majority of frugal, homemade goodies I whip up to keep my homestead clean and healthy, not only does a great job but simplifies things for me. No need to keep my cupboards stocked with a different commercial cleaner for every room, every appliance, every gadget, every surface, every THING at my homestead. I keep lots of vinegar and baking soda around, and with those I can clean ANY thing.

God always gives us just what we need, it's we who think we can outdo Him by making something "more advanced," "better," and so on. How foolish we can be.

Vin Aiger! One of the most amazing, frugal and all purpose 'natural clean' items you can have on hand is vinegar. The name "vinegar' comes from the French, and is suspected to have originated when a cask of wine cracked, and the words 'vin aiger!' were uttered at the disappointment of what would now be 'sour wine' when the cask of wine was exposed to air. Little did they know how wonderful that 'vin aiger' would turn out be.

The uses of vinegar are nearly endless. In addition to cleaning, it is an excellent for cooking, killing weeds on a hot summer day, tons of home remedies, and for home school science experiments (remember the vinegar-and-baking soda volcanoes?). The health benefits are numerous as well.

We're all familiar with vinegar as a salad dressing, and in foodstuffs; after all it is a completely natural food. However, vinegar is technically an acetic acid with a low pH, therefore has its own natural germ and virus fighting properties. Not only does it make wonderful salad dressings, it is a disinfectant, it cleans, sanitizes, has medicinal healing properties, and it's even known for killing e-coli when marinating meats.

Vinegar has been around for thousands of years. The Bible even references it. Babylonians used it as a preservative and condiment, adding herbs and spices to it. The Greeks reportedly used it for pickling vegetables and meats. During the Civil War it was used to treat scurvy, In WW1 it was treating wounds.

Can you think of anything else that can clean your toilet, soften your feet, and be a main ingredient in your next homemade salad dressing? I can't! ☺

Vinegars are very multipurpose, and do so many jobs, from the kitchen to the bathroom, and everywhere in between.

Let's start with the basics. Plain old white vinegar. I buy this stuff by the gallon(s), because it is so useful, for just about everything. It is perfect for disinfecting and cleaning, contains no toxins, no harmful chemicals, and can clean just about your whole household. Let's take a look at some of the benefits of this little miracle in a bottle.

In the bathroom, vinegar can be used full strength in a sprayer bottle on tile and grout. Spray down your tile, let it stand and grab an old toothbrush and a small cup of full strength vinegar to dip your toothbrush in, apply elbow grease, and scrub that grout to whiten and remove soap scum.

You can also use full strength vinegar on glass shower doors to remove soap scum and to remove hard water stains on fixtures and porcelain.

I like to use 1 C, dumped in the toilet, while I clean the rest of the bathroom, let it stand, and then go back to the toilet, sprinkle in some baking soda and scrub – cleans and disinfects.

Clean your showerhead by unscrewing it off the pipe, and placing it in a Tupperware® container filled with vinegar and 1 TB of baking soda (this will fizz a bit), let it set for a couple hours, rinse with hot water and screw back on the shower pipe.

Vinegar in the kitchen has endless uses. Keep an old sprayer bottle full with a half vinegar/half water mixture. This can be used to clean (and shine) glass and stainless steel.

It will clean countertops quickly, and is a wonderful de-greaser.

Full strength vinegar can be used to clean coffee pots with little effort. Fill the water compartment with vinegar, run through the brewing cycle once (or even twice), then run two cycles of fresh water to rinse.

Cleaning wood cutting boards is easy with full strength vinegar, simply wipe/scrub with the grain of the wood, rinse and dry off.

Dump a 1/2 C in your dishwasher for a sparkling and streak-free clean rinse to your dishes.

For cleaning no wax floors use 1/2 C white vinegar to a

half gallon of warm water.

To deodorize your kitchen skin drain, pour 1 C of white vinegar down the drain every few weeks.

Have a 'smell' in the 'fridge that just won't go away? Place 1 C of apple cider vinegar in it for a few days; the 'mystery smell' will be gone.

In the laundry room, you can add 1 C of white vinegar to each wash load as a fabric softener, if you prefer your fabric softener in the dryer, dump a small amount of vinegar on an old washcloth and toss in the dryer with your wet load.

Use a half vinegar/half water filled sprayer bottle to spray on stained clothing before tossing into the wash.

Clean your washer with a hot water only load and a 2 to 3 Cs of vinegar every few months – this will clean, freshen, de-grease, and disinfect your washing machine.

When you launder your shower curtain, rinse with 1 C of vinegar and hang to dry out.

When washing baby clothes (especially diapers) add 1 C of vinegar to the load – it will get rid of any smells/acid and make clothes soft and fluffy.

We exclusively line dry around our homestead, and if you're like me, you know how this can result in linty clothing if you aren't super careful about your loads, and even then sometimes we still get lint and static cling. Add 1 C of white vinegar to the load and that will all but disappear.

Vinegar Tips and Remedies

Vinegar Spray Bottles – ideally you'll want two of these at the ready – one with pure vinegar, the other with a half vinegar, half water combination. Having vinegar in a dispenser of this type makes its use much simpler in many cases.

Finding mold in the house? Use your full strength vinegar spray bottle, spray area, let set five minutes and go back with an old toothbrush or rag and scrub clean (toss the rag into the trash when done).

To remove stickers that have been used to "decorate" furniture and other surfaces, moisten with vinegar. Let sit for at least ten minutes, then remove.

For persistent room odors, place a bowl of vinegar in the room overnight.

For spills on carpet, use a sponge or cloth to soak up as much liquid as possible. Then spray with a mixture of half vinegar, half water. Let stand for about two minutes, then blot with towel or sponge. Repeat as needed.

For more persistent stains, use a mixture of 1 tsp vinegar, 1 tsp liquid dish soap, and 1 C warm water. Let stand for about two minutes, then blot with towel or sponge. Repeat as needed. When finished cleaning, dry using a hair dryer set on low.

To clean silver, pewter, copper, or brass, dissolve 1 tsp salt in one cup vinegar. Add flour to create a paste (1/4 cup or more). Apply the paste to the metal item, and let stand for at least fifteen minutes. Rinse with warm water and polish with a soft cloth.

No-wax floors can be cleaned with a solution of 1 C vinegar per gallon of water for a shinier surface.

To clean wood paneling, use a mixture of 1/2 C olive oil, 1/2 C vinegar, and 2 Cs warm water. Apply to paneling with a soft cloth. Dry with a clean cloth.

To remove corrosion or mineral buildup from showerheads, remove the showerhead, soak in vinegar overnight.

Remove stains from the toilet bowl by spraying with vinegar and scrubbing. You could also pour 1 C of vinegar in the toilet at night, (when no one is using/flushing) let stand, scrub with toilet brush in the morning.

To remove soap build-up from faucets, clean with a mixture of one part salt to four parts vinegar.

Want a sparkling tub? Use full strength vinegar on an old rag or washcloth to wipe the tub down – clean and shiny.

Spray shower walls and shower curtain with vinegar to help prevent mildew.

To keep ants away, spray vinegar along doorways, windowsills, countertops – anywhere that ants are likely to appear. If you find an ant trail (path that ants use repeatedly), clean it with vinegar.

To remove odors from the sink or garbage disposal, pour in 1 C or more vinegar. Do not rinse out again for at least an hour.

For a clogged drain, first pour in 1/2 C baking soda. Then add an equal amount of vinegar. When the mixture finishes bubbling, rinse with HOT water. (Note: some garbage disposals do not react well to this cleaning method; check with the manufacturer first.)

Remove strong odors. Rinse jars with a half and half mixture of vinegar and water to remove garlic or other strong odors. Boil water with several spoons of vinegar to remove the smell of burnt food from your kitchen.

Vinegar is an excellent cleaner for all kitchen surfaces – counters, refrigerators, stovetops.

To clean your microwave oven, put a microwave-safe bowl of 1/2 C vinegar and 1 C water in the oven, and cook long enough to boil. In addition to removing any lingering odors, this will loosen any baked-on food from the microwave's walls. (1 C of water and a TB of lemon juice will do this too.)

To remove coffee or tea stains from china, clean with a mixture of vinegar and salt.

To keep colors from running in the wash, soak in vinegar before washing.

Many persistent stains can be removed with vinegar: coffee, chocolate, ketchup, jam, cola, wine. Gently rub stain with vinegar, then wash.

To make your "brights brighter," add 1/2 C vinegar to the rinse cycle.

For fresher cloth diapers, add 1 C distilled vinegar to the rinse cycle. This will break down uric acid and remove both lingering stains and scents. Line dry in the sun for extra 'whitening,' naturally.

To remove scorch marks from an iron, rub with a mixture of vinegar and salt.

To remove soap residue from the washing machine, run an empty (no laundry) cycle with 1 C vinegar added.

To remove the smell of smoke from clothing, add 1 C of vinegar to a tub of hot water. Let clothing hang in the same room for several hours.

Keep cats away. Sprinkle vinegar on areas you don't want the cat walking, sleeping, or scratching on. To keep cats off windowsills or other surfaces, spray with vinegar. This will also keep them from scratching upholstery (spray an unnoticeable area of the fabric first to make sure the vinegar doesn't cause a stain).

To keep dogs from scratching their ears, clean with a soft cloth dipped in diluted vinegar.

If your dog should have a run-in with a skunk, vinegar will take care of the smell better than even tomato juice. Using vinegar diluted 50 percent with water, rub the dog's fur. Rinse with warm water. Repeat as needed.

Kill weeds. Spray full strength on growth until plants have starved.

Ants. Spray vinegar around doors, appliances, and along other areas where ants are known.

Polish car chrome. Apply full strength.

Keep chickens from pecking each other. Put a little in their drinking water.

Tenderize meat. Soak in vinegar over night.

Freshen vegetables. Soak wilted vegetables in 2 Cs of water and a TB of vinegar.

Boil better eggs! Add 2 TBs to water before boiling eggs. Keeps them from cracking.

Soothe a bee sting or jellyfish sting. Dot the irritation with vinegar and relieve itching.

Relieve sunburn. Lightly rub with white vinegar; you may have to reapply.

Condition hair. Add a TB of vinegar to dissolve sticky residue left by shampoo.

Fight dandruff. After shampooing, rinse with vinegar and 2 Cs of warm water.

Soothe a sore throat. Put a teaspoon of vinegar in a glass of water. Gargle and then swallow.

Treat sinus infections and chest colds. Add 1/4 C or more vinegar to the vaporizer (check manufacturer instructions/warnings on your vaporizer, first). I just put a pot of water on the wood stove and let it get hot and then add vinegar and let it release into the air.

Feel good. A tsp of apple cider vinegar in a glass of water, with a bit of honey added for flavor, will take the edge off your appetite and give you an overall healthy feeling.

Deodorize the kitchen drain. Pour 1 C down the drain once a week.

Eliminate onion or garlic odor. Rub on your fingers before and after slicing.

Clean and disinfect wood cutting boards. Wipe with full strength vinegar.

Remove fruit stains from hands. Rub with vinegar.

Cut grease and odor on dishes. Add a TB of vinegar to

hot soapy water.

Clean a teapot. Boil a mixture of water and vinegar in the teapot. Wipe away the grime.

Freshen a lunch box. Soak a piece of bread in vinegar and let it sit in the lunch box over night.

Clean the refrigerator. Wash with a solution of equal parts water and vinegar.

Clean and deodorize jars. Rinse mayonnaise, peanut butter, and mustard jars with vinegar when empty.

Clean the dishwasher. Run a cup of vinegar through the whole cycle once a month to reduce soap build up on the inner mechanisms and on glassware.

Clean stainless steel. Wipe with a vinegar dampened cloth.

Clean china and fine glassware. Add 1 C of vinegar to a sink of warm water. Gently dip the glass or china in the solution and let dry.

Get stains out of pots. Fill pot with a solution of three TBs of vinegar to a pint of water. Boil until stain loosens and can be washed away.

Dissolve rust from bolts and other metals. Soak in full strength vinegar.

Get rid of unwanted smells. Let simmer a small pot of vinegar and water solution.

Unclog steam iron. Pour equal amounts of vinegar and water into the iron's water chamber. Turn to steam and leave the iron on for five minutes in an upright position. Then unplug and allow to cool. Any loose particles should come out when you empty the water.

As you can see, vinegar has so many uses.

Baking Soda . . . the (frugal) all purpose mineral!

Sodium bicarbonate or sodium hydrogen carbonate is a white solid that is crystalline but most commonly appears as a fine powder. It has a slightly salty, alkaline taste resembling that of washing soda (sodium carbonate). It is a component of the mineral natron and is found dissolved in many mineral springs. Since it has long been known and is widely used, the salt has many related names such as baking soda, bread soda, cooking soda, and bicarbonate of soda. In colloquial usage, its name is shortened to sodium bicarb, bicarb soda, or simply bicarb. Those terms have now fallen out of common usage, so today you'll most often hear it referred to as just plain old "Baking Soda." Baking soda is a naturally occurring mineral ... thankfully so, as its uses are just about endless.

Call it what you will, it has TONS of practical uses around the home and will clean just about anything, not to mention give rise to your baking and clean your produce. Let's take a look at some of the great things baking soda can do.

Fruit and Veggie Wash – How about all those fancy schmancy produce cleaners that are now on the market to wash away the lovely pesticides that are used in growing these days? First of all, I suggest that you grow your own. But if that is out of the question, buy from a local farmer or gardener you trust not to use those types of toxins. If store-bought produce is used, use this great (cheap) spray to clean:

> Get out a clean, empty sprayer bottle, fill it with 2C clean fresh water, 3TBs baking soda and 1TB lemon juice – shake up. Spray your produce and rinse under cool, clean water. ☺

Baking Soda "Home Remedies" – Make a paste with water to use as a great toothpaste, you could also mix in a drop or two (depending on how much you are making up) of peppermint essential oil to flavor it up nicely and freshen your mouth.

Use it as an antacid, a 1/4 tsp to 1 C of water will get rid of heartburn.

Sprinkle or use powder puff on underarm area as a great all natural deodorant.

Make your own 'Homemade Baby Powder' with plain baking soda or you can mix with arrowroot powder, which I prefer (clumps up less) for a wonderfully FRUGAL baby powder.

Sprinkle 1/2 C into your bathwater and soak, to relieve sunburn, bug bites, skin irritations and such. You can do the same for baby to treat diaper rash.

Remove strong kitchen odors (onions, garlic, fish, etc.) from your hands with a baking soda paste – just scrub, rinse and the odors are gone.

All Around the Home – Baking soda can be thrown on stove fires to extinguish the flames. The carbon dioxide generated when the powder burns starves the fire of oxygen.

Sprinkle it lightly in shoes, boots – any footwear, to absorb odors and freshen.

Sprinkle in cat litter boxes to keep odors away.

Keep cut flowers fresh longer by adding 1 tsp to the water in the vase.

Wash baby toys without chemicals. Mix up a quart of warm/hot water and 4 TBs of baking soda, scrub clean, and rinse in warm/hot water.

Clean scuffs and crayon off your walls with a baking soda/water paste mixture. Gently scrub and they're gone.

Clean your BBQ grill with baking soda and a heavy duty scrub brush.

Sprinkle liberally over garage floor grease spots, scrub and rinse.

Clean out your coolers and thermoses with a hot water/baking soda solution.

Keep a small bowl or jar of baking soda in the fridge and freezers to absorb odors and moisture. Do this anywhere you have moisture, to control the humidity; stir up on occasion to maximize the life of the baking soda. It's also great in closets to get rid of any musty smells.

We sprinkle baking soda in the bottom of all our trash cans to help with odors and any possible leaks.

Sprinkle some baking soda in your veggie crisper drawer, cover with a paper towel and put your veggies in – this helps them hold their 'crispness' longer.

Soak baby clothes and dishrags in a mixture of warm water and baking soda to rid of smells.

Make a past to clean out enameled cast iron and stainless steel pots and pans.

Clean your dentures with baking soda and toothbrush.

Sprinkle a handful in the wash load to remove smells and brighten your clothes.

Sprinkle a bit of baking soda on a damp washcloth or sponge to clean kitchen countertops and the fridge.

Mix with hot water to clean baby bottles.

Clean those stale kitchen sponges by soaking in a quart of hot water and 4 TBs baking soda.

Basic 'Receipts'

Back in the 'olden days' recipes were called 'receipts.' Here are some basic 'receipts' of staple homemade cleaners I use at my homestead to keep it clean.

I use a window/glass cleaner, a scrubbing cleaner (toilets, tubs, etc), a basic all-around spray cleaner (countertops, walls, floors, appliances, etc.), a furniture oil for woods and I love to have a simmering pot of essential oils/herbs mixture on the wood stove as a lovely 'air purifier/freshener.'

Now, some basic receipts to mix up, with all the goodies in your 'Starter Kit.'

(Reminder: when I refer to the measurement of a 'dropper,' I am referring to 10 drops from the dropper of a 1 oz essential oil bottle.)

Window/Glass Cleaner – Take one empty, clean sprayer bottle and fill it with a 50/50 mixture of water and vinegar. I also like straight vinegar, too – but both work. Shake well and you're ready. Some folks use old newsprint rather than paper towels here, but beware as some newsprint contains toxic inks and chemicals. I use an old rag of sorts (I keep a small box going under my kitchen sink with cut up old clothing that has seen better days and give it new life as a cleaning cloth).

This vinegar and water solution can also be used wherever you might find mold. I tend to see it in our window tracks in the winter time. I just spray a little, then grab my old toothbrush, scrub and wipe out with an old rag. (In this case, I'll toss the rag). Add 2 droppers of peppermint essential oil to this mixture and you've got a minty fresh version of your window/glass cleaner. Not only does it smell nice, it is an effective insect repellent.

Scrubbing Cleanser – I love this one! Fill a pint or quart size canning jar about 3/4 full of baking soda and use a straw or a chopstick or butter knife to create holes in the baking soda for essential oils. (If you have stains you're dealing with, use one part Borax and two parts baking soda.) Mix in around 20 drops of lavender essential oil (or tea tree, lemon, or orange), put the lid on and shake well. Then use a small nail to punch about five decent sized holes in the lid; you'll have your own "shaker" of cleaner that contains NO chlorine or chemicals and works even better than the smelly commercial version. I use this to scrub my stainless steel kitchen sink, bathroom sinks, and our shower with one of those green scrubbie pads. Want a sparkling tub? Use full strength vinegar on an old rag or washcloth to wipe the tub down – clean and shiny. To remove water spots from glass shower doors, do the same and rinse with plain water.

"Soft Scrub" – You'll want to gather up an old Tupperware® with a lid to house this wonderful soft scrub. You'll add in a 1/2 C baking soda, and enough Castille soap (I like Dr. Bronner's) to make a thick consistency (think frosting), then add in 5 drops of an antibacterial essential oil. I like tea tree, lavender, lemon or rosemary; add what you like or blend a few together to get a scent you enjoy. Scoop a bit on a sponge and wash the surface you are cleaning and rinse. Simply clean!

All Around Spray Cleaner – I use this everywhere. Take one of your empty, clean sprayer bottles and fill 3/4 full with water. Add one full dropper (adjust as necessary according to your supplies) of grapefruit seed extract (I buy mine at 'More Than Alive' and it's called 'Grapefruit Seed Crush' there). Now add a dropper of lavender essential oil and shake well. I clean my appliances and my countertops with this and get those little fingerprints off of walls; it even does kitchen and bathroom floors. Just spray it on the floor and mop up or use one of those handy old rags – get it a bit wet and wipe up. It really is 'all purpose'!

Furniture Oil – I've seen lots of recipes for this, but the most effective and frugal one I've found for my wood furniture is plain old olive oil in a half pint canning jar. Fill to about 3/4 full and add 20 drops of sweet orange or lemon essential oil. Shake it up, dab a bit on a rag and polish up your woodwork. This one smells great, and works even better.

Homemade Air Freshener – I like to keep an old pot on the wood stove with water and a few drops of essential oils and herbs in it. They fill the house with such a lovely aroma. I love myrrh, eucalyptus and lavender. I have a cassia essential oil and cinnamon stick blend I make up, too – more on that later.

Homemade Spray Air Freshener – Spray air fresheners are very popular; however, they are chock full of toxic air pollutants. Make your own natural air freshener.

Get an empty, clean spray bottle; fill 3/4 full with distilled water and add your choice of essential oils. It's that simple. I use a 12 oz spray bottle and approximately 30 drops of a combination of essential oils. I love to use straight frankincense and myrrh essential oil, and spray it directly on my bedding, too. Just shake it up and spray to enjoy a clean natural fragrance.

Beyond the Basics

As you get more comfortable making your own homemade concoctions, you can add more ingredients to your "Starter Kit," to expand your ability to create more recipes. I would suggest a wider variety of herbs and essential oils. Just make sure you're using essential oils, NOT fragrance oils. Essential oils are what you'll want for true cleaning, disinfecting, and taking advantage of the natural properties of these oils. Here is a list of just a few of the many essential oils that have great cleaning properties, in addition to their naturally beneficial therapeutic health properties: lavender, citrus (lemon, lime or sweet orange) tea tree, eucalyptus, rosemary, peppermint, clove, cinnamon, and citronella. I also love to use cedar, hyssop, myrrh, and frankincense and myrrh.

A few herbs you might want on hand? Well, it's nice to have a variety of fresh herbs growing in the windowsill for culinary purposes. I like to have some dried herbs for making up bath and body products, too. You can start with rose petals, lavender, chamomile, and rosemary, just to name a few. You can order a variety of quality dried herbs from many sources online; take a look at the resources list at the back of this book. This is also easily done yourself. Pick the fresh leaves a few at a time and tie with kitchen string and hang til dry – or use a dehydrator.

You may want to add some other items to your homemade cleaning line up, such as Fels-Naptha® old fashioned bar soap and Arm and Hammer® washing soda for making your own laundry soap. How about some castile soap or glycerin for making your own liquid dishwashing soap and many other products? Make sure to always have a fresh lemon or two on hand; lemon juice is a great cleaner and full of natural antibacterial properties. You can really customize your ingredients list to your own family. Try out the following recipes or create your own. The only limits to what you can do with your homemade products are your needs, imagination, and preferences.

In the Kitchen

Keep your kitchen and everything in it sparkling clean with some of these simple recipes.

Dishwashing Liquid
  1/4 C Soap Flakes
  1½ C HOT Water
  1/2 C Glycerin
  1/2 tsp Lemon Essential Oil
  1 Clean Squirt Bottle (16 oz)

Grate up any bar of pure soap (homemade soaps are my personal preference here, but a bar of Ivory®, Fels-Naptha®, or something similar will do). Pour the soap flakes and hot water into a pitcher, stirring until the soap has dissolved. Let cool about 5-10 minutes. Then stir in your lemon essential oil and glycerin. (Sweet orange or lavender essential oil would be great here, too.)

The mixture will start to thicken into a gel; pour it into your squirt bottle and use 2 TBs per dishpan of hot water to clean your dishes.

"Essential" Dishwashing Liquid
22 oz Liquid Unscented Castile Soap
    (brand of your choice)
20 Drops of Lemon Essential Oil
10 Drops Sweet Orange Essential Oil
5 Drops of Grapefruit Seed Extract

Add the oils to the soap in the 22 oz plastic flip top container. Shake well to blend and add 1 TB to warm dish water. If it does not lather for you as much as you would like, add 2-3 TBs of baking soda to your warm water and swish the water to form suds.

Oven Cleaner – Put 1 C ammonia in a small bowl, and leave it in a cooled, closed oven, overnight. The next morning, remove and toss the ammonia. Wipe down the inside of your oven with a damp sponge, paper towels or old rags dipped in baking soda. Simply clean!

Microwave Cleaner – We've all but banned the microwave around here, but it IS good for heating up our wheat berry heating pads, so of course we like to keep it fresh and clean. One way to do this very simply is to take a small microwavable bowl and put 1/2 C water and 1/4 C lemon juice in it. Cook on HIGH for 3-4 minutes, allowing condensation to form on the inside of the microwave. When it's done, remove the bowl (VERY carefully, it WILL BE HOT!) and wipe down the interior of the microwave with an old rag. Voila! Clean.

Sparkling Sink – This works GREAT. Remember your scrubbing cleanser from the basics recipes? Shake a little of this in the sink; scrub with one of those green scrubbies and you will have a sparkling CLEAN sink. Another great idea to sparkle and clean the sink is to quickly scrub around it with a green scrubbie and then just wipe down with a vinegar soaked sponge. Easy.

Scouring Powder – Looking to remove stains from non-porous surfaces in the kitchen or bath? This works wonderfully, much safer for you and your family, and much more economical than those chemicals on the market. Grab a plastic container with a lid that seals tightly and combine:

1 C Baking Soda
1 C Borax
1/2 C Table Salt

Mix together well. To clean your stained surface, simply sprinkle some of your powder onto a damp sponge or directly on the surface that needs cleaned, scrub, rinse, and dry.

Secret All Purpose Kitchen Weapon – This one is so easy and chock full of good ol' common sense. Did you know that if you have extremely HOT or even boiling water, you can dip a portion of an old rag or washcloth in it and clean just about anything? Seriously, try it. If I am boiling water, when I am done, I will do a couple things: first off I will grab a washcloth and dip a bit of it in the hot water (being careful, obviously it is hot – don't ask me how I made this discovery). I look around for sticky fingerprints on our walls, or sticky counters, or the high chair – the possibilities are endless. Boiling hot water will clean up just about any gross, sticky messes with EASE. If you don't have little ones running wild through your home creating sticky fingerprints or messy high chairs, another thing you can do is wipe out/down the fridge/freezer. I can just about always find some drops of spilled juice or a bit of sticky jam on a countertop, and the fridge can always use a quick once over, inside and out. A hot, damp cloth will make it very simple. Grab 1/2 C of baking soda and dump it down the kitchen sink; follow it with the remainder of the boiling water to rinse. This not only cleans out the disposal area of the sink, but washes down through the pipes, keeping them cleaned out, too.

Cleaning the Disposal – Do you have a garbage disposal? They can be a blessing or a curse. To keep yours in top working condition, turn on the disposal and toss 3-5 ice cubes down, along with 1 C of vinegar. Do this every few weeks or so. I also have heard of folks making vinegar ice cubes just for this purpose. This will clean it out, rid the disposal of smells, and sharpen the blades, all at once.

Mop That Floor – I've seen folks do this in such a variety of ways. With an ol' fashioned wringer mop, to a towel on the floor, to a scrub brush, sponge mops – you name it. I can't tell you HOW to mop; only that we all know it needs to be done, and there is a great non-toxic, water based solution to clean it with. Run a gallon of warm/hot water in the sink or in a bucket; add 2 droppers of grapefruit seed extract. Stir and mop/clean the linoleum floors in kitchens and baths. It works wonderfully.

The Laundry Room

There are so many easy ways to frugally and naturally clean the family's clothing. Just a few simple ideas? Keep a bottle of plain old white vinegar in the laundry area to save a TON on all those commercial fabric softeners. Wash in cold water when you can to save on the electric and water bills. Keep some baking soda in the laundry area; it's a natural water softener and has excellent whitening power.

Take care of the washing machine, too. Run a load of hot water and vinegar every few months to keep the washer clean and grime free. Line dry when the weather allows; try a wooden wash rack to dry inside when it doesn't. Little things will add up to savings over time, not to mention the health benefits. Essential oils in the laundry can have so many pluses. Not only will essential oils add some fantastic, therapeutic scents to your laundry, they can kill germs and bacteria, whiten, remove stains and more.

You can so easily create your own essential oil blends for

your laundry. Have someone in the family (or the whole family?) with a cold or flu? Wash their bedding with a dropper of eucalyptus oil added. Did you know you can spread flu, even chickenpox via the laundry?

When someone is getting sickly, try washing all loads with eucalyptus and even tea tree to get rid of those unwelcome germs. Tea tree oil in the wash has a variety of benefits.

Have someone that suffers from recurring yeast infections? Add a dropper of tea tree oil to the wash loads. Two droppers of tea tree oil to a load of bed linens will also get rid of dust mites who love to live in our bedding. As an antifungal and antibacterial, tea tree oil is great on a wash load of baby's diapers.

Looking to just add a nice scent that has great all around properties (antifungal, antibacterial, calming, relaxing therapeutic properties)? Try a dropper of lavender essential oil. I love to use a lavender/rose geranium blend when I am doing a load of skirts and dresses for us girls.

Looking for a more manly scent? Try a cedar essential oil.

Use ylang-ylang, rose, or another romantic floral to wash delicates and undergarments. Essentials add so many benefits. Chamomile is soothing; a lavender-chamomile blend is wonderful for everyone's bedding and beneficial for a good peaceful sleep; sweet orange helps remove stains and whiten. I use one dropper as my own rough estimate measurement on the amount I use; you may want to use less or more. That's part of the beauty of making your own ~ you customize your use to your preferences. I also add my oils to the wash load once the washer has filled with water, so they aren't put directly on cloth; you could put your essential oil/blends in the softener dispenser instead.

One of the simplest, yet large differences, I have made to our family's clean routine is in our laundry soap. Everything we wash touches us in some fashion, and the chemical residue of commercial laundry products is absorbed into us through our largest organ: our skin. This was one of the first big changes we made years ago; it's healthier, simple to do, and cheap.

This is a very easy recipe, with great results and I can adjust it as needed for my family. I tend to add a dash or so more Borax or washing soda, as my husband comes in with grease and dirt on his clothes more often than not, and these products are great degreasers. This recipe is literally foolproof, because no matter how I've messed it up, it always gets our clothes clean.

Homemade Laundry Soap: First, find a big old pot. (I have an old one used specifically for making soaps/cleaners – I have written CLEANERS on it with a marker and put up high on a shelf in the laundry room – no one will be mistaking it, and accidentally cooking food in it.)

Add to the pot: 4 Q water.
    Then put this on the burner, medium heat:
    1/2 C 20 Mule Team Borax® (sodium borate)
    1/2 C Arm and Hammer Washing Soda® (sodium carbonate)
    Stir….then add 1/3 to 1/2 C Grated Bar of Fels-Naptha®.

You can usually find Borax, Fels-Naptha or Washing Soda at your local Mom and Pop grocery store. (Note: washing soda is not the same as baking soda.) Fels-Naptha®, it seems, is getting harder to find these days BUT, it can be found at www.homesteadoriginals.com.

Now, heat on medium high at this point and stir (again, with a spoon just for your cleaners-not cooking) until it's dissolved. This will then need to cool down (an hour or so), and then we'll pour 1/3 into each of our 3 old laundry soap/fabric softener containers (100 oz size). Fill the remainder of each with HOT water, put the lid on tight and shake thoroughly. That's really about it.

This recipe will generally gel up and become quite thick, so that is why I like to put it into old laundry jugs. They have a tight fitting lid and I can shake it up or add more hot water if needed. Old gallon milk jugs or an old bucket (with lid) will work here, too. You really can't mess this soap up – it IS that easy. If it's really thick, add some more hot water and shake it up. If it's really runny, I just call it a "learning experience" and use a bit more in each load with that particular batch of laundry soap – it will still get your clothes clean.

Occasionally I will add a little lavender or a favorite essential oil or blend for a little light fragrance or special property I want the oil to add to the laundry soap. Otherwise there is not a whole lot of scent to this, which can be nice, too. I usually eyeball my measurement into the wash, but approximately a 1/2 C works very well, and gives a nice clean to the clothes without the chemical residue that commercial brands leave behind. This amount will last us our family of five a month or more, including washing cloth diapers almost daily, give or take. I don't strictly measure for each load, but it ranges in price from one to three cents per load. You can't beat that for a healthy laundry soap.

Laundry Helps and Tips . . . Make your own Dryer Sheets, Fabric Softener and MORE

Line Drying – Hanging our clothes on the line not only gives them a nice clean scent, but saves the wear and tear on electric dryers, and saves energy (and that electric bill).

Be sure to keep your line dried clothes just as soft as if they went through the electric dryer by adding 1 C vinegar to the rinse cycle of each load you'll be hanging out to dry. Hanging clothes on the line also uses the natural whitening power of the sun to diminish stains. This is especially good on whites, linens, and baby's diapers. You can even dry on a wooden rack in the winter; we set ours up near the wood stove and it works great.

Homemade Dryer Sheets – This is a great way to use up old cloth, and cotton rags or scrap clothing. Take your piece of cloth and add 5 drops of your favorite essential oil to it. (No more than this or you could end up with staining of your clothing in the load and have to re-wash.) These can be reused, too, by just adding a couple more drops of the essential oil to the cloth each load; you can recycle it back through the wash to be used again and again. Here are a few ideas for making your own blends for your home-made dryer sheets: rosemary and thyme for a natural, earthy scent; lavender and chamomile for a relaxing, sooth-ing effect; sweet orange and lemon for a refreshing scent; eucalyptus and peppermint (or just the eucalyptus) for cold/flu sufferers; ylang-ylang and jasmine for a romantic floral scent.

Making your own Fabric Softener – These are for the washing machine and are such a money/health saver. Here are a few different recipes. Try them out and see which you prefer.

In a large plastic container with tight fitting lid, add 4 C of water to 2 C of baking soda. Then add 2 C of vinegar (very slowly or the mixture will foam and bubble up on you). Use 1/4 to 1/2 C per load.

How about a citrusy fabric softener? Lemon scents just

say FRESH and CLEAN to me. Try this recipe if you are a lemon lover.

Combine the following in a heavy duty plastic container, or even a pitcher for easy pouring: 10 C vinegar, 1 C water, 1 C baking soda, and 30 drops of lemon or lemongrass essential oil. Mix thoroughly and use 1 C per load in the rinse cycle.

The easiest fabric softener? Add 1 C of white vinegar to the rinse. Looking for a bit of lovely fragrance in your fabric softener? Take your gallon jug of vinegar and add 25 drops of lavender essential oil to it.

How about this one? Take your gallon jug of vinegar and add 15 drops of peppermint essential oil to it. This will fight tough odors, too.

Spray Starch – Combine 1 C Water, 2 TBs Cornstarch (you could add a couple drops of your favorite essential oil here as long as it's clear oil) in a sprayer bottle; shake up well before each use.

Remove crayon stains from clothing by using an old toothbrush and vinegar. Dip toothbrush in vinegar and scrub; wash as normal.

Wash denim inside out to avoid fading, and on its own to save wear and stains on your other clothes.

Blood stains can be removed with a mixture of: 1 teaspoon of hydrogen peroxide and 1/4 teaspoon of clean household ammonia. Just mix these 2 ingredients in a small bowl and rub right on the stain; when the stain begins to fade, rinse and launder as usual.

Whiten up those yellowed whites. Take 1 C of vinegar and 10 C hot water (very warm – not boiling) and put into a bucket and mix. Soak your yellowed whites overnight and launder in the morning.

Shop/Outdoor Clothes? Borax is an excellent grease cutter and cleaner of grimy, greasy, smelly workin' clothes. Add 1 C to a load of these type clothes to get really clean.

Tomato sauce stains? Soak your stained garment in a dishpan or bucket of 3 C warm water + 1 C hydrogen peroxide for 30 minutes.

NOTE: Never combine chlorine bleach with ammonia, vinegar, or lemon juice. Extremely toxic fumes will be produced!

The Homestead Bath

We all appreciate a nice clean bathroom, especially when we want to indulge in a hot, relaxing bath. Keep your homestead bath sparkling clean with these recipes.

No Scrub Toilet Cleaner – Flush the toilet to wet the entire bowl. Sprinkle 1 C Borax all around inside the bowl, and then pour a 1/2 - 1 C of vinegar all around. Let it sit undisturbed overnight and voila, clean! If you have heavy stains, a bit of scrubbing may be required.

Heavy Duty Toilet Scrub – Combine 1 C Borax and 1/2 C of lemon juice to form a paste. Apply this to the toilet bowl using an old rag, or sponge; let set a few hours and scrub off; flush.

Scrubbing Cleanser – This is our "old reliable" from your "Basics" list. Fill a pint or quart size canning jar about 3/4 full of baking soda and use a straw or butter knife to create holes in the baking soda for essential oils. (If you have stains you're dealing with, use one part Borax and two parts baking soda.) Dump in around 20 drops of lavender essential oil (or tea tree, lemon, or orange), put the lid on and shake well. Then use a small nail to punch about five decent sized holes in the lid; you'll have your own shaker of cleaner that contains NO chlorine or chemicals and works even better than the smelly commercial version. I use this to scrub my stainless steel kitchen sink, bathroom sinks, and our shower with one of those old green scrubbie pads.

Want a sparkling tub? Use full strength vinegar on an old rag or washcloth to wipe the tub down – clean and shiny. To remove water spots from glass shower doors, do the same and rinse with plain water.

Multipurpose Bathroom Cleaner – Combine 2 TBs Borax, 1 TB washing soda, 2 TBs lemon juice, 5 TBs vinegar, and 3 C of hot water in a clean sprayer bottle. Shake it up until all your ingredients have mixed together and spray away. This will work great as an all purpose disinfectant cleaner, especially on tile and ceramic surfaces.

Daily Shower Cleaner – Grab a sprayer bottle and mix up: 1 C of vinegar, 1/2 C water, 15 drops of orange essential oil, and 10 drops of lemon essential oil. Spray this all over the shower after each use and it will keep the shower clean and sparkling in between heavy duty cleanings.

Shower head Cleaner – We have heavy mineral deposits here at our homestead and this works great to clean and unblock our showerheads. Over the sink or tub pour 1/2 C of baking soda, and 1 C vinegar into a an old freezer bag or even an large old Tupperware® container. Wait a minute for the foaming to stop and put the open end of the bag over the showerhead (which should be covered by the solution) and tie to the showerhead stem with a piece of twine or ribbon; you could also use tape or a large twist tie. You can also unscrew and remove the showerhead and put into the Tupperware® container. Let it soak for an hour; remove and clean with hot water and a clean cloth.

Drain Cleaner – Commercial drain products are some of the most toxic products out there. Keep those products out of your home by using this simple recipe. Pour 1/2 C of baking soda down the drain, followed by 1 C vinegar, let set a few minutes and follow it with boiling water to rinse. This not only cleans out the drain, but also helps eliminate odors, and the proper pH of the septic system. Repeat every two weeks or as needed.

Rust Remover – Squeeze the juice of 1 lime over your rust spots, then cover that moistened area with 1/4 C table salt. Let sit for a couple hours and then scrub with an old green scrubbie pad and rust will be gone. Depending on how deep the rust is, you can always scrub with a stainless steel scrubber and that alone may just do the trick.

Septic Tank Helpers – No one wants septic tank troubles. Every month, flush 1-2 TBs of baker's yeast down the toilet. This will keep the septic system dissolving those solid wastes and that's just enough said there. You can also take a couple Cups of regular sugar, toss in a saucepan or pot with 1 Q water, simmer until sugar is dissolved, and cool. Add in your 1/4 C cornmeal and 1 TB yeast, mix and take the whole thing to the bathroom and flush it. This is best done at night, when no activity will be going on in the bathroom. I've also been told by my septic guy that flushing a cup of yogurt once a month is helpful.

All Around the Homestead

Here are a wealth of natural cleaners, tips and helps for use all over the home. Everything from keeping your home smelling lovely on the inside with natural homemade potpourri blends, to natural weed killers and car wash soap for the outside.

Indoors

You can easily grow your own herbs and flowers for homemade potpourri blends, as well as cooking, making more homemade, natural clean products, sachets, dried flowers, medicinal products – lots can be done with your own little herb garden. This can be done indoors with just a few pots, all year long. Growing indoors keeps the indoor air cleaner, and can add nice scents to your home as well. You could also extend this to outdoors in the proper season for your area, and dry your herbs and flowers for future use too. Looking to add some lovely fresh fragrance to the air in your home? Depending on preference, there are a variety of ways to do this. Take one or two cotton balls and put your favorite essential oil on them. Toss those into your vacuum cleaner bag as you are changing it. You could even put a few drops right onto the bag itself. When you vacuum, the lovely scent is released. Simple!

If you have an oil burner, put in some olive oil or your preferred carrier oil and add in a few drops of your favorite essential oil.

I just about always have a pot of water on our wood stove to keep moisture in the air, but I love to add in some goodies to keep the air fresh and working for us. I use this pot just for this purpose, and use essential oils, herbs, flowers and homemade potpourri blends. It lends such a nice homey feeling with such great scents wafting about – I'll share a few of my favorites with you.

Homestead Potpourri – Fill one big ol' pot with water. Toss in 10 or so cinnamon sticks, about 3 tsp of ground cinnamon, some crushed cloves (about 2 tsp), some orange and/or lemon peel, and some fresh apple peelings. (You can do cinnamon oil, clove oil, lemon and/or sweet orange essential oils here, too.) Simmer on the stove and enjoy. I love this one.

Winter Cold Blend – When colds and flu abound in the winter, I put eucalyptus essential oil as well as Frankincense and myrrh essential oil in my oil burner, but get a batch of my Winter Cold Blend going in my big ol' pot.

Fill your big ol' pot with water.
   Add: 2 Droppers of Eucalyptus Essential Oil
   5-10 Drops of Peppermint Essential Oil
   1 Dropper of Lavender Essential Oil
   5 Drops Tea Tree Oil
   5 Drops Clove Oil

Let it simmer and fill the air. You could also modify this recipe and use any of these you have on hand. This makes for a great steam treatment blend, too.

Special Blend – You could simmer this blend in a pot of water, make sachets, or just set out in a pretty dish or bowl.
1/2 C Rosemary Leaves
1/2 C Peppermint Leaves
1/2 C Eucalyptus Leaves (torn up or you can use euca
    lyptus essential oil sprinkled on the dried matter)
1/4 C Thyme
1/8 C Whole Cloves
2 TBs Grated Lemon Peel
2 TBs Grated Orange Peel

Cinnamon Stick Fall Blend – You could simmer this blend in a pot of water, make into herbal pillows, or sachets, or just set out in a pretty dish or bowl.
10 Cinnamon Sticks
1/2 C Whole Cloves
1 Bay Leaf
1 tsp Cinnamon (ground)
2 C Apple Slices and Peelings (must be dried)
1 C Orange Peel (fresh or dried)

Summer Garden Blend – Combine all these in a glass canning jar with lid and shake around often, cap and set in a cool, dark spot, shaking/stirring jar every so often. Let it set for about a month to cure or blend. Then, once cured you can simmer in a pot of water, or set out in a pretty bowl or dish.
1 C Rose Petals
1 C Calendula Flowers
1 C Snapdragon Flower Heads

1/2 C Sunflower Petals
1/2 C Marigold Flower Heads
1/2 C Statice Petals
1/2 C Cedar Chips

Winter Wonderland Blend – Mix all ingredients together and put into a Ziploc® type bag for 24 hours. You could set this blend out in a pretty dish or bowl, or simmer in water on a hot stove.
1 C Evergreen Needles
1/2 C Dried Apple Pieces
1 C Cedar Chips
1 C Cinnamon Sticks (broken up)
1/4 C Whole Cloves
1 TB Chopped Gingerroot
1 TB Cinnamon (ground)
10 Drops Frankincense Essential Oil

Sleepytime® Blend – This makes for a great night's sleep when sewn into an herbal pillow, too; you can make into sachets, or just set out on your nightstand in a pretty bowl.
1 C Chamomile Flowers
1/2 C Sweet Marjoram
1 C Lavender Buds
1/2 C Sweet Clover Flowers
1/2 C Lemon Balm Leaves
Drizzle 1 Dropper of Lavender Essential Oil on the dried matter.

Herbal pillows and sachets are so simple to make. Just sew together any double layered cloth into a square pillow (or whatever shape you prefer), stuff and stitch up. Sachets can even be made by putting your dried stuffing right in the middle of a piece of cloth, draw the sides up all around and tie with a ribbon, twine, string, whatever you prefer – as long as it doesn't come loose, and is dried thoroughly before using, you're set. You can also make or buy little organza drawstring bags for cheap – they really allow your sachet stuffing to breathe and are very pretty. You can tuck your sachets in linen closets, dresser drawers, under pillows and sheets, hang in closets, wherever you'd like. These make lovely gifts as well. Sachet ingredients can be as simple as lavender buds, rose petals or you can create your own recipe/blend. Here are a few ideas:

Clothes Keeper
2 C Cedar Chips
1 C Sandalwood Chips
1/2 C Dried Sage
10 Drops Patchouli Essential Oil

Lovely Linens
2 C Lavender Buds
1/2 C Lemon Balm
1 C Rosemary Leaves
1 C Rose Petals
10 Drops Lavender Essential Oil
5 Drops Rosemary Essential Oil

Outdoors
How about some Natural Clean helps for outdoors around the home? Here are some ideas for you.

Prevent your garden tools from rusting. Take a bakery bucket or any bucket, fill 3/4 with sand, add 1 quart of olive oil and mix together. Push your large tools like shovels and rakes into the mixture to prevent rusting when not in use.

This is a great idea for storing your tools over the winter season.

Looking for an all natural weed killer? Grab your trusty gallon jug of vinegar (or a smaller spray bottle of full strength vinegar) and dump or spray directly on the weeds on a nice sunny day; repeat as needed. I will often use a few gallons over the course of a spring/summer season. You could do the same with full strength bleach too, just be extra careful that children and critters can't get near the area you're treating.

Make your own natural homemade insecticide. Gather up 5 cloves of garlic, 1 TB of olive oil, 2 C of hot water and 1 TB dishwashing soap. Start by getting out the blender to puree your garlic with your olive oil, strain this mixture into a quart or larger canning jar (canning jars make great strainers. Use quart canning jars, lids and basket style coffee filters, works great). Then add your water and homemade dishwashing soap, put the lid on tight and shake up to mix. Transfer this into a sprayer bottle and use on indoor or outdoor plants that have been invaded by pests.

Looking to keep critters out of your trash cans? Douse the outside of the cans with ammonia. We do this every few weeks or so, with a Cup or two of ammonia and NEVER have had critters getting into our trash cans.

Flies Be Gone! During the summer months especially, going out to the barn to milk in the late afternoon/early evening can just be miserable with all the flies. Keep a sprayer bottle handy filled with 1/2 water, 1/2 apple cider vinegar and 3 FULL droppers of eucalyptus oil. Shake and spray; the flies stay away.

Got Ants? Want to get rid of them? I've used a few things with good success. If it's dry out (no rain), sprinkle cinnamon around entry points of doors and windows. I've also made up a sprayer bottle 3/4 full of water and 1 dropper of peppermint oil. I spray this around indoors on countertops and such if I see those little sugar ants on my counter, or outdoors on the decks – they'll suddenly disappear.

Keep spiders away with a sprayer bottle mixture of water and a dropper of peppermint essential oil; spray around indoors and out.

No one wants fleas! Keep them at bay with these simple tips: Grind up fennel seed and place anywhere you want fleas gone. Doghouse, dog bedding, in front of doorways, in kids' play areas, indoors and out. Add a dropper of tea tree oil in Fido's bath water; you can add a teaspoon of apple cider vinegar to animals' drinking water to repel fleas, too.

Keep deer away from the garden. Deer do not like deodorant soaps. Keep those scrap pieces of deodorant soap or chop up pieces of a bar, put pieces into old socks, tie shut, and tie with string or twine around (every 5-10 feet apart) your garden area you want protected. Replace as the rain and elements deplete the soap.

Other Animal Treatments. Rub a little cornstarch into Fido's coat before brushing and it will help remove those mats and tangles easily. This works great for our feline friends too. Cedar chips under Fido's bed will help keep fleas at bay and rosemary or eucalyptus leaves under Kitty's bed will do the same.

Remember that most essential oils will kill cats, so keep all those away from your feline friends.

Natural clean for the CAR?

Absolutely! Keep your vehicle clean inside and out with these simple recipes.

Car Wash Soap. Get a big bucket, toss in 1/2 C dishwashing liquid (see recipe under Kitchen) and 1 gallon warm to hot water, mix and wash up the exterior of your vehicle.

Citrus Car Wash: You'll need a big bucket, 1 gallon of warm water, a 1/4 C or so of our homemade dishwashing liquid (see recipes under Kitchen), and 2 droppers of lemon or orange essential oil. Mix everything together in your bucket and wash away. Rinse well.

To keep the **interior carpets** naturally clean, too, make up this homemade upholstery shampoo. You'll need 1/2 bar of Fels-Naptha® (grated), and 2 TBs Borax. Mix together in a large bowl and slowly add in one pint of boiling water; stir well, let cool, then whip with a fork or old eggbeater and brush the suds into your upholstery/soiled areas. Remove by wiping off with an old rag or damp sponge.

Looking for a natural clean for your **vinyl and leather interiors**? Grab a small plastic Tupperware® and mix in 2 TBs Murphy's Oil Soap (this is a vegetable based soap), 4 TBs olive oil, and 1 dropper of lemon or lavender-lemon essential oil. Mix up well, apply with an old rag or sponge and wipe clean with rag or old soft washcloth. SO easy!

Clean the **battery terminals**, and keep that battery in working order. Combine a 1/2 C baking soda and a dropper of orange essential oil, along with enough water to make a paste. Grab an old toothbrush to apply the paste to the terminal with, and scrub away. When done, wipe the terminal clean with a damp rag, then a dry one and toss them both when done.

Have an **oil spill** from the car or other homestead machinery? Combine 5 C natural kitty litter, 1 C baking soda, 2 droppers peppermint essential oil. Mix well, sprinkle over spill and let set for a few days. Sweep up and toss what remains.

Homemade Clean & Healthy for the Body

There are so many simple, yet truly luxurious ways to keep our bodies clean, healthy and taken care of with natural ingredients. Not to mention the commercial counterparts cost an OUTRAGEOUS amount of money, and are chock full of 'not good for us' stuff. Dyes, chemicals, synthetics...the list is long. I'll show you how to make your own and customize exactly what you want in your bath and body products.

To get started, you'll want to gather up some basics to make your own **Homemade Clean Health & Beauty Starter Kit**. You probably have quite a few of these in your pantry already:

Beeswax (I prefer the little pellets versus blocks)
Olive Oil
Coconut Oil
Shea Butter
Arrowroot Powder
Baking Soda

Vinegar
Oatmeal
Honey
Cornmeal
Powdered Milk
Sea Salt
Epsom Salt
Witch Hazel
Lavender Buds
Lavender Essential Oil
Peppermint Essential Oil

Of course as you experiment and expand your recipes, you'll want to add to my 'basic' list here.

Some of my Favorites.

Mama's Homemade Lavender Baby Powder – For years now, I've made up my own homemade baby powder, it is so very simple, frugal and quite heavenly. You'll need:

One canning jar with lid set up
Small whisk is helpful, too.
Arrowroot powder
Baking soda
Lavender essential oil
Screwdriver (old Phillips, smallish-medium head)
Optional: dried lavender and/or rose petals and canning
    funnel

Get out all your supplies and ingredients before you start. I try to make this up in a somewhat quick manner so my oil won't clump up with my dry ingredients. I shake it up at the end, too, and have learned to keep that in mind when judging my headspace.

I lay down a towel or cloth to catch any spills, put my canning jar on it, place my funnel in my jar. I then get out all my supplies: arrowroot, baking soda, and lavender essential oil. I have used arrowroot powder ONLY, but I tend to sprinkle in a few tablespoons of baking soda along the way, too; the mixture just yields a better end result.

I have the same quart jar I've used to make my powder in for about five years now, a quart – this is TOTALLY forgiving, use whatever sized jar you want. I then go about layering my ingredients into the jar. I'll sprinkle in a couple TBs of baking soda, 1/2 cup to a full cup of arrowroot powder, and 5 drops of my lavender essential oil, repeat until my jar has about 2 inches of headspace left. It is BEST if you can use a small whisk to 'whisk together' each layer – this way your essential oil doesn't 'clump up' with your other ingredients, and you'll get a nice mixture.

Now – you could also layer in crushed dry material such as your organic rose petal or organic lavender buds, they will have to be very finely crushed to release their wonderful properties (make sure you are using organic dried herbal matter, commercially grown rose petals, especially, can be sprayed with tons of toxins) – and to fit through the holes you are going to make in your jar lid.

If I am in a creative mode, I'll make up a little extra batch for just the girls in our homestead, that has crushed rose petal and even some Rose of Sharon essential oil from Israel.

So, now that you have your jar filled, you whisk the whole mixture very gently OR if you do not have a small whisk – you can and put your lid set up on, and shake it up really thoroughly (just be sure to leave that headspace for shaking up). Then, VERY carefully, I take my lid off, set it on my old towel or cloth and use the screwdriver to poke holes thru the lid (obviously don't do this on your kitchen countertops) to make my own 'shaker jar.' I tend to do this on my wooden cutting board.

This really is a NICE powder – gentle enough for baby's skin (test it out, some children might have some allergic reaction – so test first) but adults love it, too – you could even get creative and make it up as gifts. It gets REQUESTED by my family . . . I just love that!

Homemade Lip Balm – Care for those lips with this easy to make, moisturizing, handcrafted lip balm. Just gather up empty lipbalm sticks or small cosmetic 'pots' or tins and your ingredients and you're set.

1/8 C Beeswax Pastilles
1/2 C Olive Oil
1 tsp Raw Honey or Vitamin E Oil
Peppermint Essential Oil or Extract (this varies upon personal preference, I like to add add about 10 drops; customize to your liking or not, it's completely optional).

Melt your beeswax, then add your olive oil and honey (honey doesn't combine very well – FYI) or Vitamin E oil. Stir to combine, remove from heat, add peppermint if desired and pour into your chosen containers. Let cool and harden. ENJOY.

Homemade "Vaseline®" – This is a great recipe and it just does not get any easier. With 2 ingredients . . . and the approximately 2 minutes it takes to make; you can't go wrong, not to mention the results are amazing. I use this as you would a 'vaseline®' type product, however I LOVE it as a hand and foot lotion too – takes a minute to absorb into the skin and does a great job of relieving dry skin. I will often put it on before bed and let it really soak in overnight. I love this stuff!

Gather up one half-pint canning jar, regular mouth lid (I prefer the plastic ones for homemade goodies such as this) and whatever pan (stainless is best here, definitely no Teflon®) you will melt your ingredients in. I use a little 2 cup stainless measure 'pan' which makes it really easy.

Ingredients:
1/2 C Olive Oil
1/8 C Beeswax

Pour these in your pan, melt on low heat until completely melted together, remove from heat.

Pour into your half-pint canning jar, just let it stand until cool and hardened up, then put your lid on and label. I include the recipe on the label when it will fit, and in this case, it sure does. That way, I (or my children) can make again, simply – the recipe is right there.

This is a perfect example of how absolutely simple, pure, and frugal making your own homemade health and beauty products can be.

Homemade "VaporRub®" – I will use my "Homemade Vaseline®" recipe as the base for making my own Homemade VaporRub®, it's so simple. Prepare the "Homemade Vaseline®" only add in a 'pinch' more beeswax. Get the consistency YOU want. You can always remelt your oil/beeswax and add more oil to soften up, more beeswax to harden up. When you remove from heat, add in 30 drops of eucalyptus essential oil and 15 drops of white camphor essential oil. Use just as you would any other chest rub. Remember, as with anything else we make or use; watch for reactions, test a small area of skin first.

'Bugs Be Gone®' Spray – This is so easy to make at home, the results are excellent, and you don't have all the nasty toxins and chemicals you get with commercial 'bug sprays.' Fill a clean sprayer bottle with witch hazel (12 oz), add in 20 drops of citronella essential oil and 20 drops of lemongrass essential oil. I also add in 10 drops of either tea tree or geranium essential oil (to keep ticks off). Shake it up and spray it on any exposed areas (arms, legs, etc.). If you are in tick country, use around ankles and head / neck areas liberally, but do not spray in face or eyes. Try a tiny bit on your children first to make sure they have no allergic reaction to the essential oils (adults, too). This is also great to spray around the area where you are sitting outside. I love this!

The BEST Handcrafted Lotion Bars – My daughters and I started making these and just LOVE them. Not only are they fun to make together, they are really simple, frugal, and I love that the girls even research what essential oils to add to their lotion bars for a certain desired effect. Unlike liquid or gel lotions, lotion bars do not contain any water, alcohol, or other undesirable ingredients. Lotion bars are pure oils, rubbed on the skin to soothe and heal. You can make them plain, or with essential oils; either way the results are lovely. You will need equal parts of natural beeswax, as well as a liquid oil and a solid oil. There are a lot of options for your liquid and solid oils, again it is all in your personal preference; customize to your liking.

I recommend olive oil or apricot kernel oil for your liquid oil. You could use almond oil (watch out for those with nut allergies if you are sharing or gifting your lotion bars) or a primrose oil. (I do not recommend canola or vegetable oils; I try not to eat them, so I surely don't want them on my skin.)

For solid oils, I prefer coconut oil or shea butter; you can also use cocoa butter, and I've also used palm kernel oil (this will generally come in a flake form). So let's gather up our supplies and make lotion bars. You'll need:

1 C Organic Beeswax Pastilles (little pellet form vs. block)
1 C Olive Oil /Liquid Oil
1 C Coconut Oil /Solid Oil

Pour all ingredients in a double boiler and melt together, slowly stirring. Once melted and combined, remove from heat. At this point add in your essential oils of choice. We love Rose of Sharon essential oil, myrrh, or Lily of the Valley essential oil; add up to 30 drops of your favorite. You can experiment and add less or more essential oil, mix and match essential oils to create your own special blend customized for your needs.

Pour into a mold of your choice, into greased stainless muffin tins, even ice cube trays, plastic craft molds, square baking dish; whatever you choose. Once they have hardened, we pop our molds in the freezer for a few minutes, then take them out and your lotion bars will pop right out of the molds. Some folks say to warm up your molds, I have found that just popping them in the freezer works great. If you choose to pour into a large square baking dish, you can easily cut into bars by heating up a stainless steel knife blade and cutting through. Be sure to store your finished product in a sealed container out of any direct sunlight, out of hot vehicles, and away from any heat source. These are a lot of fun to make and even nicer to ENJOY!

Simply Wonderful Homemade Calendula Salve – Springtime finds us enjoying much more time outdoors; however that also means bug bites, scrapes, cuts, and probably a few bruises, too! You can very simply make your own all natural, healing calendula salve and you'll be back outside enjoying the season in no time.

Having an all-purpose salve on hand is essential. I keep this salve made up and on hand year round, and if anyone in the family has any type of ailment you'll hear someone say, "Get some salve on it!"

Calendula, is technically known as *calendula officinalis*. 'Calendula' is from the Latin 'kalendae,' the given name from the Romans, used to indicate how it bloomed year round in their area. And 'officinalis' means it is included in official lists as a medicinal herb. Another more common name for calendula is pot marigold; and it has some pretty amazing healing properties. This powerful, yet pretty 'flower' is from the asteraceae family; other family members include yarrow, arnica, and chamomile, which are all powerhouse herbs. Calendula is both a culinary and medicinal herb. The petals are completely edible and are great on a fresh green salad. I tend to use dried calendula for medicinal uses, primarily for its anti-viral and anti-inflammatory properties. It is also great in tinctures, poultices, in teas: it really is wonderfully diverse.

However, as with any herb or commercial medicine, if you are pregnant or nursing always check with your doctor first. I also recommend with any commercial or herbal preparation that you do a small test before using in full capacity, especially with children. Test a bit of salve on a small patch of skin to assure no allergic reactions. So with all the formalities out of the way, let's gather up our supplies make some of this wonderful healing salve.

Here's what you'll need: One quarter cup dried calendula petals, one-half cup extra virgin olive oil, one eighth cup grated beeswax or beeswax pastilles, thirty drops lavender essential oil, cheesecloth, heavy pot and spoon, measuring cup, rubber band, Crock-Pot® (paper coffee filters and canning jars, too, depending on your preference and on which way you choose to make your salve. I also like to double or triple this recipe; it keeps well and I never (well, almost never) run out.

I have made this salve for years, and done some variations (occasionally adding in a handful of plantain leaf, comfrey, or lavender buds) and sometimes amending the preparation method, too. The addition of lavender adds another layer of protection (kills many common bacteria) as well as a pain reliever. Comfrey is a very powerful herb commonly used in poultices for blunt trauma injuries; broken bones, burns,, and in the case of my salve I use it for its ability to heal swollen bruises. Plantain is sometimes referred to as the 'mother of all herbs' and I can see why; it works healing wonders on just about any medical problem. I will add a handful of plantain leaf to my infusion for its ability to heal bites, stings, cuts, wounds, bee stings, and so much more.

I obtain most of my essential oils at Mountain Rose Herbs: http://www.mountainroseherbs.com. If I have not grown my own herbs, I will get them at Mountain Rose or at More Than Alive: http://www.morethanalive.com.

I most often make my salve using solar infusion. I will put olive oil and calendula petals in a canning jar, put the lid on and set in out in the hot afternoon sun. However, there have been times where I've run out and need to make a batch faster, or there is no "hot afternoon sun." In that case I will put my olive oil and calendula petals in a small Crock-Pot® and heat on low for approximately three hours. When either of these processes is complete, I will generally use a canning jar covered with an inverted paper coffee filter, secured with the canning jar band, and slowly pour the infusion in, straining out the calendula petals. I prefer this method for smaller batches, because there is less mess. If I am doing a larger batch, I lay cheesecloth over the top of a glass measuring cup (I use a four-cup Pyrex® measure that has a very wide mouth) and secure the cheesecloth with a strong rubber band. Then I slowly pour the olive oil through the cheesecloth so the petals are caught on top and the oil filters through into the measuring cup.

Next I pour my strained oil into a heavy saucepan (stainless steel; no Teflon®) and turn the heat on low. I add the beeswax and stir occasionally until melted. Once the beeswax is completely melted, I remove the saucepan from the heat, let sit a couple minutes and add the essential oil(s), stirring to distribute these throughout the mixture (chopsticks or popsicle sticks are great for this). Then I pour the mixture into a clean container. I use small tins for carrying in purses or backpacks, and I include these in all our first-aid kits. I use larger canning or glass jars for general use around the house.

I leave the salve uncovered until completely cooled, label and cap it. Prepared and stored properly it will last upwards of a year – if it doesn't get used up faster. Just rub on as needed.

I love making this for my family, I love knowing what is in it (no chemicals or toxins) and I absolutely LOVE using what God gave us to take care of our bodies.

Makeup Remover – If you wear makeup, here is a simple, yet effective way to remove it . . . naturally.
1 C Distilled Water
1/2 tsp Dr. Bronner's Unscented Castile Soap
1 tsp Olive Oil

Combine all ingredients in a glass container with lid. Shake it up, apply to a cloth of cotton ball and wipe off make up and residues.

Another great way to remove makeup is pure jojoba oil.

Natural Hair Care . . .
Keep Your Tresses Looking Their Best

Make your own Handcrafted Shampoos, Conditioners and Herbal Rinses.

Herbal Shampoo – This is a nice shampoo, that really works well, we find we don't even need a rinse or conditioner after using. Here is what you'll need:

8 oz or so of Distilled Water
1 TB of Dried Rosemary and 1/2 C of Dried Rose Petals
    *Optional 1 TB of Dried Sage - especially
            nice for dark hair and/ or scalp issues.
3 TBs Liquid Castile Soap
3 TBs Aloe Vera Gel
1/4 tsp of Jojoba Oil
20 to 30 Drops of Pure Rosemary Essential Oil

This WORKS great, no toxins and SUPER SIMPLE to

make. I pick up all my ingredients on the cheap (and great quality) at Azure Standard or over at Mountain Rose Herbs and whip up my own, E A S Y.

Start out with a clean quart jar. Boil the water, dump the dried herbs in the jar, and pour the boiling water over the top. Put a lid on it and let it sit at least an hour, or even overnight.

Next you'll strain the herbs out (I use paper coffee filters, but you could also use cheesecloth).

Once strained, I dump it into an old shampoo bottle and add my remaining ingredients. A small funnel is really handy at this step; then put the lid on, shake up and it's done.

You have just made your own homemade shampoo – and we absolutely LOVE this recipe. Now, you CAN use regular water in this recipe, if you don't have distilled on hand – it just has a bit shorter shelf life. However, that is a non-issue more often than not, as this will last at least 6 months. Shake it up well each time you use it and I use about a quarter to fifty cent piece sized amount in my cupped hand in the shower (it is a lot more 'liquid-y' that the thick stuff you find at the store) and it works great – AND no conditioner needed, either.

What I really love is the ability to personalize this recipe. You can (as noted above) add sage – or a slew of other herbs to change the properties and results you get. Here are a few ideas:

Have blonde hair and want to highlight that? Add chamomile or calendula. Dark hair lends itself to sage, or even nettle. If you have oily hair go a bit less on the oils. If dandruff is a problem substitute tea tree instead of rosemary essential oil. Enjoy lavender essential oil and lavender buds? Add it in, just stick with the basic formula of dry matter and oils listed in the recipe . . . the options are endless and the price is nice, too. Make it extra inexpensive and dry your own organically grown lavender and rose petals from your garden.

Simply Refreshing Homemade Shampoo – I love peppermint, it wakes me up and is so invigorating. Whip up a batch of this homemade shampoo and start your mornings off right:
> 1/4 C Distilled Water (regular filtered water is fine – just not as long a 'shelf life')
> 1/4 C Liquid Castile Soap, Unscented (I use Dr. Bronner's "Baby Mild" version)
> 2 tsp Jojoba Oil
> 1/8 tsp Peppermint Essential Oil
> 1/8 tsp (I use a little less) Tea Tree Essential Oil

Mix all ingredients together in an old shampoo bottle or other bottle, then add another 1/4 C distilled water and you're set – homemade shampoo in seconds, with no toxins.

Natural Deep Conditioner
> 1 Avocado (mashed)
> 1 TB Olive Oil

Mix avocado and oil together thoroughly, and massage mixture into hair and scalp. Put hair up in a plastic shower cap or wrap with plastic wrap for about 15 minutes and rinse well, clean/shampoo hair as normal. This makes a wonderful deep conditioner.

Homemade Vinegar Hair Rinses – Vinegar beauty treatments? Absolutely! Vinegar makes the most fantastic hair rinse. We truly over wash/treat our hair with all the daily shampooing, conditioning, hair drying, hair sprays, gels, colorants, etc. Apple cider vinegar tends to work best on the hair and a cup of it in the shower rinsed through our hair is a perfect, simple clean. You can also make up herbal rinses with vinegar to treat oily hair, dandruff, dry hair – even add dark or light 'highlights' naturally.

Vinegar rinses are great for itchy scalp, dull hair and they help to restore the natural balance and acid in the scalp, not to mention that healthy shine. If the vinegar smell is not appealing to you (actually, after you rinse well, it's not a strong smell at all) you can add a few drops of your favorite essential oil, too.

I start with a clean, quart-sized canning jar and fill 1/2 to 3/4 full of apple cider vinegar. From there, depending on what type of rinse I want to make, I add my herbs:

For Dandruff
1/4 C Chamomile
1/2 C Sage Leaf
1/4 C Rosemary
1/4 C Thyme

For Oily Hair
1/2 C Rosemary Leaf
1/2 C Yarrow Leaf

For Dry Hair
1/2 C Calendula Flower
1/2 C Nettle Leaf
1/4 C Marshmallow Root

For Golden Highlights
1/2 C Calendula Flower
1/2 C Chamomile

For Dark Highlights
1/2 C Sage Leaf
1/4 C Comfrey Leaf
1/2 C Black Walnut Hull (chopped)

Once my herbs are in, I put my lid/ring on firmly, shake it up and set in a sunny windowsill for a week or two. (This is known as "solar infusion.") Give it a shake once a day or so. When I am ready to use it, I strain out the herbs (by using another canning jar, coffee filter, or cheesecloth and ring), put it into a plastic container, place in the shower, and it's ready to use. I always have a batch of one of these mixtures brewing on a windowsill somewhere in the house.

For a 'Salon Conditioning Treatment' try this home-made recipe:

Mix 3 eggs, 2 TBs olive oil, 1 tsp vinegar, and apply to your hair. Cover with a towel or one of those cheapie plastic shower caps for a half hour. Rinse in the shower, with 1 C apple cider vinegar and VOILA . . . clean, conditioned, shiny hair.

Skin care...keep your skin soft and clean with these homemade recipes

You can't beat the price either, when compared to the overpriced stuff at the cosmetic counter.

For the Face

Oatmeal, Cream, and Honey Facial Mask

1/4 C Organic Heavy Cream or Goat's Milk Cream
1/4 C Organic Ground Oatmeal
1 TB Organic Honey

Combine all ingredients in a bowl/container; let set for 15 minutes until it thickens up a bit, then massage on face and neck, and let it dry for 20 minutes and rinse.

Favorite Toner – Make your own facial toner with witch hazel. This is a super frugal way to create your own toner.

Grab a wide mouth pint or half-pint canning jar (or whatever container you prefer) and fill 3/4 full and add in 10 drops lemon essential oil for the half-pint / 20 per full pint and mix. Make sure you test a small patch of skin first. It's a refreshing toner at a FRACTION of the price the stores fetch and it works wonderfully.

Chamomile Skin Toner
1/2 C Dried Chamomile
2 C water
1 C witch hazel

3 Drops Lavender Essential Oil for Normal Skin
3 Drops Lemon Essential Oil for Oily Skin
3 Drops Geranium for Dry Skin

Get a clean glass canning jar with lid (or other tight lidded container) ready with a basket style coffee filter and canning jar ring to secure it. Boil your water, turn off heat, and add chamomile. Cover to steep for 10-15 minutes. Strain, and let cool. Add your witch hazel and essential oil of choice, put your lid on and shake up well. Let stand at room temp for 24-48 hours. Ready to enjoy. Clean face daily with your homemade toner and cotton ball, avoiding the eyes.

Cornmeal and Honey Scrub
1 C Honey
1 C Organic Cornmeal
1/2 C Water

Mix your honey and cornmeal together well, then slowly mix in water to get the consistency you want. You might want to add a little more water, or a little less depending on your preferences. We make this up and place in an old canning jar and just scoop out what we want to give our faces a nice exfoliating scrub. It's gentle enough to use every day.

Heavenly Body/Skin Care

Body Scrub – You can make your own body scrubs, so SIMPLY. Body scrubs remove excess dead skin that clog pores and leave our skin feeling rough; especially wonderful for rough feet, elbows, and knees. Body scrubs follow a basic foundational recipe, and from there you can customize.

1 C Sugar, Sea Salt or Brown Sugar
1/2 C Oil (olive, almond, melted coconut oil, etc.)
20 Drops of Essential Oils (your choice - optional)
1/2 tsp Vanilla Extract (optional)

Facial Scrub – To make a facial scrubs, mix ground oatmeal, cornmeal, or oats with a little water or milk until a paste forms. Apply in circular motions, staying clear of the eyes. Leave to sit for a minute of two and rinse off with warm water.

Scrubs work best when applied to damp skin. Never use scrubs on broken skin or skin that is wind-burned or sunburned.

Lavender and Milk Bath Sachet

1/4 C Dried Lavender Flowers
1/4 C Instant Powdered Whole Milk

Place into a muslin drawstring bag. Toss the bag into the

bath water while it's running. You can also use the bag to rub your skin as you bathe.

Oatmeal Skin Soother
1/2 C Organic Oatmeal
1/4 C Instant Powdered Whole Milk

Place ingredients into a muslin drawstring bag. (You could use just oatmeal here, too.) Toss the bag into the bath water while it's running. Use the bag to rub your skin as you bathe. This works for babies with diaper rash to older children and adults with eczema; very soothing to the skin.

Gentle Milk Bath
1/2 C Powdered Milk
1/4 C Cornstarch
Your Favorite Essential Oil (couple drops - optional).

Add all your ingredients into a glass canning jar with lid, screw on tight and shake it up (if you get clumps, break them up with your fingers.) Run your warm bath water and toss in about a ½ C per bath. Leaves skin silky and soft. Make up a double or triple batch of this – enjoy. For gift giving, customize the oil to the person and decorate up your jar with fabric over the lid and a nice ribbon.

Heavenly Homemade Herbal Bath Bag – Grab a large square of cheesecloth or an old clean flour sack and fold into a large square. Grab a handful of dried herbs of your choice (lavender, rose petals, chamomile, lemongrass, sage, peppermint, etc.) and place in the middle of your cloth. Gather up the corners and tie it up securely and toss it in the bath. Use as a giant herbal washcloth on the skin, too.

Bath Soak
1/4 C Sea Salts
1/4 C Epsom Salts

Dump directly under warm/hot running water as you fill your tub. You can add in a few drops of lavender essential oil, eucalyptus or your favorite, too.

Cold/Flu Bath Soak
10 Drops Eucalyptus Essential Oil
1/4 C Sea Salts
1/4 C Epsom Salts

Dump directly under warm/hot running water as you fill your tub.

Natural Perfume Solid
2 oz Jojoba Oil
1 oz Beeswax
15 Drops Ylang-Ylang Essential Oil
10 Drops Patchouli Essential Oil

In a double boiler over low heat, gently melt jojoba oil and beeswax; add essential oils, stir, and remove from heat. Pour a bit into your container (you could use small tins, pots, even a tiny Tupperware®) to let it cool and test it first before you pour your whole batch. You can always go back and re-melt your ingredients to liquid form and add more oils or different oils to your liking, and then cool and re-pour. This is one you can get really creative with. I enjoy using a geranium and Rose of Sharon essential oil blend. I love to make this versus wear synthetic perfumes. It's not only fun to make, but nice to wear, too. Just dab on pulse points.

Just for Hands . . . our hands are always exposed to the elements, pamper them

The Toughest Homemade Hand Cleaner
1/4 C Fels-Naptha®* (grated)
2 TBs Fine Sand or Pumice
1 C Water
Plastic Container (2 C size)

Place soap and water in an old pan. Place over low heat; stir until soap is melted. After mixture cools, add the sand or pumice. Store in your plastic container. Just dip fingers into soap mixture and lather hands as needed and rinse well.

*Any grated bar of soap will work, but I find Fels-Naptha® works great.

Remember, if you can't find Fels-Naptha® at your local grocery store, Homestead Originals has it for you.

Old Fashioned Gardener's Hand Scrub
1 C Grated Soap
2 TBs Borax Powder
1 TB Powder Pumice (you could also substitute a little
   fine sand here)

Mix all ingredients together in a plastic container or jar. To use just scoop out a small amount and mix with a bit of warm water in your hands and start scrubbing. You could follow this up with a TB of olive oil in your hands to rub off those last little bits of dirt and grime. The olive oil makes a great skin conditioner and will leave hands very soft.

Super Clean Hand Scrub – Just take a 1/4 C of cornmeal, add in enough apple cider vinegar to moisten and scrub up, rinse in cool water.

Natural Hand Sanitizer – Mix up all these ingredients, put into a spray pump top or smaller squirt type bottles; shake up and you are ready to sanitize your hands the natural way!

1/4 C Aloe Vera Gel
1/4 C Witch Hazel
1 tsp Vegetable Glycerin
1 TB Apple Cider Vinegar
10 Drops of Tea Tree Essential Oil
Your Favorite Essential Oil (a few drops - optional)

Homemade "Vaseline®" – I have this recipe in the 'My Favorites' section of the book, too, but I just had to put it here as well – this is such a treat for the hands!
   This is a great recipe and it just does not get any easier! With two ingredients . . . and the approximately two min-

utes it takes to make; you can't go wrong, not to mention the results are amazing. I use this as you would a 'vaseline®' type product, however I LOVE it as a hand and foot lotion, too – takes a minute to absorb into the skin and does a great job of relieving dry skin! I will often put it on before bed and let it really soak in overnight. I love this stuff!

Gather up one half-pint canning jar, regular mouth lid (I prefer the plastic ones for homemade goodies such as this) and whatever pan (stainless is best here, definitely no Teflon®) you will melt your ingredients in. I use a 2 C stainless measure 'pan' which makes it really easy!

Ingredients:
1/2 C Olive Oil
1/8 C Beeswax

Pour these in your pan, melt on low heat until completely melted together, remove from heat.

Pour into your half-pint canning jar, just let it stand until cool and hardened up, then put your lid on and label. I put the recipe right on the label, when it will fit, and in this case, it sure does! That way, I (or my children) can make again, simply – the recipe is right there!

This is a perfect example of how absolutely simple, pure, and frugal making your own homemade health and beauty products can be.

Tired, Sore, Troubled Achy Feet?

Foot cures can be natural, too! Try a foot bath and then follow up with the foot massage oil right before bedtime to allow the oil time to get deep into the skin! This will work wonders for folks with athlete's foot, too!

Foot Bath
1/2 C Sea Salt
5 drops of Geranium Essential Oil

Fill a shallow wash tub or large plastic bowl with warm water, add the salt and geranium oil, and stir until salt dissolves. Soak feet for up to 15 minutes, and dry WELL.

Foot Massage Oil
1 TB Olive Oil
5 drops Geranium Essential Oil

Mix the oils together and massage into each foot before bedtime.

Foot Soak – Fill a large bowl with white vinegar, add in 10 drops of lavender essential oil, mix. Soak feet 15 minutes – enjoy!

Foot Powder
1 C Baking Soda
1/2 C Cornstarch
1 C Arrowroot Powder
10 drops Tea Tree Essential Oil
15 drops Lavender Essential Oil

Combine all ingredients in a container with a tight fitting lid; shake up very well to be sure oils are mixed thoroughly. This is not only a nice treat for the feet – it helps prevent foot odor and infections. Sprinkle in shoes and/or socks.

Peppermint Foot Rub
1 C Coconut Oil
15 drops Peppermint

Mix softened coconut oil with peppermint essential oil, place in a wide mouth jar (easy to get back out when you want it). Note that coconut oil gets very hard in less than 'warm' temperatures, so keep at room temperature to make it easy to use. This foot rub is so nice, especially if you have someone else giving you the foot rub!

More Clean & Healthy Recipes & Tips

You can make anything you need at home, from natural ingredients – try some of these!

Natural First-Aid Antiseptic Ointment – Make your own homemade antiseptic ointment that is packed full with natural germ-killing properties that will help treat everyday minor cuts, scrapes, and abrasions. I love what essential oils do for us, naturally:

Tea tree oil is antibiotic, anti-fungal, antiviral, antibacterial

Lavender is an analgesic (for pain relief), antibiotic, antifungal, antiviral, antibacterial

Lemon is antibiotic, antifungal, antiviral, antibacterial

You use this just as you would a tube of commercially-prepared brands. It's even better because YOU made it, so you know what is in it!

1 1/2 oz beeswax - grated or pastilles
1 C olive or coconut oil
1/4 tsp Vitamin E oil
1/2 - 1 tsp tea tree oil
20 drops lavender essential oil
10 drops lemon essential oil

Melt your beeswax and oil together over very low heat, in a small pot or double boiler. Remove from heat and add Vitamin E oil and essential oils. Stir. Pour mixture into small sterilized jars (I love to use small canning jars or tins). Allow to cool on counter, then store in a cool, dark place. Use as needed on wounds. This will keep for nine to twelve months!

Baking Soda Beautifying Treatments – These are some super frugal treats for your skin – all with simple baking soda!

Baking soda on its own makes for a great exfoliating skin rub! Just shake a bit on a wet washcloth and scrub away! For a baking soda "facial," just make up a small batch of three parts baking soda/one part water paste and exfoliate your face/skin in the shower by gently rubbing on skin!

Baking Soda Foot Soak – Add 3 TBs baking soda to a large bowl or basin of warm/hot water and put your feet in for 10 minutes!
Add a cup of baking soda to your bathwater to soften your skin.

Homemade Toothpaste – Keep toxic fluoride out with this handcrafted toothpaste – SO simple!

1TB baking soda
1 or 2 drops of peppermint essential oil (food grade)
Enough water to make a paste

Dab a bit on your toothbrush and you're set! Make this up in bulk in a container with a tight fitting lid; it keeps nicely and works beautifully!

Organic Apple Cider Vinegar has some excellent health and nutritional benefits, too! Try these simple 'home remedies'!

Keep a small jar of it in the medicine cabinet for an aftershave to keep skin soft. Just splash on after shaving.

Fill a jar of half apple cider vinegar/half water to use as a toner/astringent to control problem skin/pimples (try this first on a small patch of skin to be sure it doesn't irritate the user's particular skin type).

Soothe a bee sting by dumping vinegar on the sting, it not only soothes but stops the itching and irritation.

Relieve dry and itchy skin by adding a couple of tablespoons of vinegar to your bathwater.

Create a great foot soak to soften your feet by filling a bucket or large Tupperware® bowl with 2 gallons of warm water and 1 Cup of vinegar; soak 30 minutes. You should be able to easily remove dead skin cells and callused areas with a pumice stone.

Using & Caring for What He's Given

These are some of my favorite recipes for frugal, natural, homemade cleaning and bath and body products. As you can see, with some basic ingredients, you can create everything you need to keep your family clean and healthy. I love that theses recipes are so easily customized to our own family's needs. A little practice making them yourself and soon you'll be creating your own custom recipes yourself. We can create our own homemade cleaners; they are so easy to make and use.

Our Heavenly Father has provided so many amazing herbs, natural compounds and such, not only for wonderful medicinal and culinary uses, but to keep us clean and healthy! By creating our own home and body care products with what He has provided, we are being good stewards of the resources He's given us.

We are making a choice each day. God is the giver of all good things, he takes care of us, gives us what we need; He is the Creator and Giver of Life.

We can choose Him and what He gives . . . life.

Or . . . we can choose man's ways, man's 'things' . . . but man's ways lead to death.

I'll take door #1.

As the Homekeeper and Helpmeet to my family, the family my Heavenly Father knit together, that He gave me the honor and blessing to care for, love and serve – it is my heart's desire to serve them in the best way possible! I believe that taking the time and love to create my own homemade products for my family is one way I can do just that!

~ Lisa

Resources

Homestead Originals: Get Fels-Naptha® Soap here, along with lots of wonderful treats for your homestead and those in it! All natural beeswax candles, biblical healing and anointing essential oils, handmade wheat berry heating pads, books, homestead skills DVDs, grain mills, and so much more! Visit: *www.HomesteadOriginals.com*.

More Than Alive: Get grapefruit seed crush here, along with a host of other goodies, including: beeyoutiful vitamins and supplements, great books, herbs, essential oils, Berkey water filters and more!

Mountain Rose Herbs: A wonderful selection of herbs, oils, teas, and goodies!

RESOURCES FROM HEALTHY LIFE PRESS

Unless otherwise noted on the site itself, shipping is free for all products purchased through *www.healthylifepress.com.*

 **We've Got Mail: The New Testament Letters in Modern English – As Relevant Today as Ever!** by Rev. Warren C. Biebel, Jr. – A modern English paraphrase of the New Testament Letters, sure to inspire in readers a loving appreciation for God's Word. (Printed book: $9.95; PDF eBook: $6.95; both together: $15.00, direct from publisher; eBook reader versions available at *www.Amazon.com*; *www.BN.com*; *www.eChristian.com*.)

Hearth & Home – Recipes for Life, by Karey Swan (7th Edition) – Far more than a cookbook, this classic is a life book, with recipes for life as well as for great food. Karey describes how to buy and prepare from scratch a wide variety of tantalizing dishes, while weaving into  the book's fabric the wisdom of the ages plus the recipe that she and her husband used to raise their kids. A great gift for Christmas or for a new bride. (Perfect Bound book [8 x 10, glossy cover]: $17.95; PDF eBook: $12.95; both together: $24.95, direct from publisher; eBook reader versions available at *www.Amazon.com*; *www.BN.com*; *www.eChristian.com*.)

 **Who Me, Pray? Prayer 101: Praying Aloud, for Beginners**, by Gary A. Burlingame – Who Me, Pray? is a practical guide for prayer, based on Jesus' direction in "The Lord's Prayer," with examples provided for use in typical situations where you might be asked or expected to pray in public. (Printed book: $6.95; PDF eBook: $2.99; both together: $7.95, direct from publisher; eBook reader versions available at *www.Amazon.com*; *www.BN.com*; *www.eChristian.com*.)

My Broken Heart Sings, the poetry of Gary Burlingame – In 1987, Gary and his wife Debbie lost their son Christopher John, at only six months of age, to a chronic lung disease. This life-changing experience gave them a special heart for helping others through similar loss and pain. (Printed book: $10.95; PDF eBook: $6.95; both together: $13.95; eBook reader versions available at www.Amazon.com; www.BN.com; www.eChristian.com.)

About the author and his message: Danish philosopher Søren Kierkegaard wrote, "A poet is an unhappy being whose heart is torn by secret sufferings, but whose lips are so strangely formed that when the sighs and the cries escape them, they sound like beautiful music...." Gary A. Burlingame is one such being, with this difference – once unhappy, due to the loss of a son, his broken heart now sings, because he kept walking by faith. His readers are the beneficiaries of the work of the One who binds up the brokenhearted, turns mourning to joy, and sets captives free.

After Normal: One Teen's Journey Following Her Brother's Death, by Diane Aggen – Based on a journal the author kept following her younger brother's death. It offers helpful insights and understanding for teens facing a similar loss or for those who might wish to understand and help teens facing a similar loss. (Printed book: $11.95; PDF eBook: $6.95; both together: $15.00; eBook reader versions available at *www.Amazon.com*; *www.BN.com*; *www.eChristian.com*.)

In the Unlikely Event of a Water Landing – Lessons Learned from Landing in the Hudson River, by Andrew Jamison, MD – The author was flying standby on US Airways Flight 1549 toward Charlotte on January 15, 2009, from New York City, where he had been inter-

viewing for a residency position. Little did he know that the next stop would be the Hudson River. Riveting and inspirational, this book would be especially helpful for people in need of hope and encouragement. (Printed book: $8.95; PDF eBook: $6.95; both together: $12.95, direct from publisher; eBook reader versions available at *www.Amazon.com*; *www.BN.com*; *www.eChristian.com*.)

 **Finding Martians in the Dark – Everything I Needed to Know About Teaching Took Me Only 30 Years to Learn**, by Dan M. Biebel – Packed with wise advice based on hard experience, and laced with humor, this book is a perfect teacher's gift year-round. Susan J. Wegmann, PhD, says, "Biebel's sardonic wit is mellowed by a genuine love for kids and teaching. . . . A Whitman-like sensibility flows through his stories of teaching, learning, and life." (Printed book: $10.95; PDF eBook: $6.95; Together: $15.00; eBook reader versions available at *www. Amazon.com*; *www. BN.com*; *www.eChristian.com*.)

Because We're Family and **Because We're Friends**, by Gary A. Burlingame – Sometimes things related to faith can be hard to discuss with your family and friends. These booklets are designed to be  given as gifts, to help you open the door to discussing spiritual matters with family members and friends who are open to such a conversation. (Printed book: $5.95 each; PDF eBook: $4.95 each; both together: $9.95 [printed & eBook of the same title], direct from publisher; eBook reader versions available at *www.Amazon.com*; *www. BN.com*; *www.eChristian.com*.)

The Transforming Power of Story: How Telling Your Story Brings Hope to Others and Healing to Yourself, by Elaine Leong Eng, MD, and David B. Biebel, DMin – This book demonstrates, through multiple true life stories, how sharing one's story, especially in a group setting, can bring hope to listeners and healing to the one who shares. Individuals facing difficulties will find this book greatly encouraging. (Printed book: $14.99; PDF eBook: $9.99; both together: $19.99, direct from publisher; eBook reader versions available at *www.Amazon.com*; *www.BN.com*; *www.eChristian.com*.)

You Deserved a Better Father: Good Parenting Takes a Plan, by Robb Brandt, MD – About parenting by intention, and other lessons the author learned through the loss of his firstborn son. It is especially for parents who believe that bits and pieces of leftover time will be enough for their own children. (Printed book: $10.95
each; PDF eBook: $6.95; both together: $12.95, direct from publisher; eBook reader versions available at *www.Amazon.com*; *www.BN.com*; *www.eChristian.com*.)

Jonathan, You Left Too Soon, by David B. Biebel, DMin – One pastor's journey through the loss of his son, into the darkness of depression, and back into the light of joy again, emerging with a renewed sense of mission. (Printed book: $12.95; PDF eBook: $5.99; both together: $15.00, direct from publisher; eBook reader versions available at *www.Amazon.com*; *www.BN.com*; *www.eChristian.com*.)

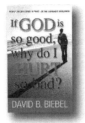

If God Is So Good, Why Do I Hurt So Bad?, by David B. Biebel, DMin – In this best-selling classic (over 200,000 copies in print worldwide, in five languages) on the subject of loss and renewal, first published in 1989, the author comes alongside people in pain, and shows the way through and beyond it, to joy again. This book has proven helpful to those who are struggling and to those who wish to understand and help. (Printed book: $12.95; PDF eBook: $8.95; both together: $19.95, direct from publisher; eBook reader versions available at *www.Amazon.com*; *www.BN.com*; *www.eChristian.com*.)

The Spiritual Fitness Checkup for the 50-Something Woman, by Sharon V. King, PhD – Following the stages of a routine medical exam, the author describes ten spiritual fitness "checkups" midlife women can conduct to assess their spiritual health and tone up their relationship with God. Each checkup consists of the author's personal reflections, a Scripture reference for meditation, and a "Spiritual Pulse Check," with exercises readers can use for personal application. (Printed book: $8.95; PDF eBook: $6.95; both together: $12.95, direct from publisher; eBook reader versions available at *www.Amazon.com*; *www.BN.com*; *www.eChristian.com*.)

The Other Side of Life – Over 60? God Still Has a Plan for You, by Rev. Warren C. Biebel, Jr. – Drawing on biblical examples and his 60-plus years of pastoral experience, Rev. Biebel helps older (and younger) adults understand God's view of aging and the rich life available to everyone who seeks a deeper relationship with God as they age. Rev. Biebel explains how to: Identify God's ongoing plan for your life; Rely on faith to manage the anxieties of aging; Form positive, supportive relationships; Cultivate patience; Cope with new technologies; Develop spiritual integrity; Understand the effects of dementia; Develop a

Christ-centered perspective of aging. (Printed book: $10.95; PDF eBook: $6.95; both together: $15.00, direct from publisher; eBook reader versions available at *www.Amazon.com*; *www.BN.com*; *www.eChristian.com*.)

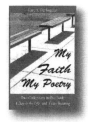 **My Faith, My Poetry**, by Gary A. Burlingame – This unique book of Christian poetry is actually two in one. The first collection of poems, A Day in the Life, explores a working parent's daily journey of faith. The reader is carried from morning to bedtime, from "In the Details," to "I Forgot to Pray," back to "Home Base," and finally to "Eternal Love Divine." The second collection of poems, Come Running, is wonder, joy, and faith wrapped up in words that encourage and inspire the mind and the heart. (Printed book: $10.95; PDF eBook: $6.95; both together: $13.95, direct from publisher; eBook reader versions available at *www.Amazon.com*; *www.BN.com*; *www.eChristian.com*.)

On Eagles' Wings, by Sara Eggleston – One woman's life journey from idyllic through chaotic to joy, carried all the way by the One who has promised to never leave us nor forsake us. Remarkable, poignant, moving, and inspiring, this autobiographical account will help many who are facing difficulties that seem too great to overcome  or even bear at all. It is proof that Isaiah 40:31 is as true today as when it was penned, "But they that wait upon the LORD shall renew their strength; they shall mount up with wings as eagles; they shall run, and not be weary; and they shall walk, and not faint." (Printed book: $14.95; PDF eBook: $8.95; both together: $22.95, direct from publisher; eBook reader versions available at *www.Amazon.com*; *www.BN.com*; *www.eChristian.com*.)

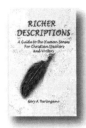

Richer Descriptions, by Gary A. Burlingame – A unique and handy manual, covering all nine human senses in seven chapters, for Christian speakers and writers. Exercises and a speaker's checklist equip speakers to engage their audiences in a richer experience. Writing examples and a writer's guide help writers bring more life to the characters and scenes of their stories. Bible references encourage a deeper appreciation of being created by God for a sensory existence. (Printed book: $15.95; PDF eBook: $8.95; both together: $22.95, direct from publisher; eBook reader versions available at *www.Amazon.com*; *www.BN.com*; *www. eChristian.com*.)

Treasuring Grace, by Rob Plumley and Tracy Roberts – This novel was inspired by a dream. Liz Swanson's life isn't quite what she'd imagined, but she considers herself lucky. She has a good husband, beautiful children, and fulfillment outside of her home through volunteer work. On some days she doesn't even notice the dull ache in her heart. While she's preparing for their summer kickoff at Lake George, the ache disappears and her sudden happiness is mistaken for anticipation of their weekend. However, as the family heads north, there are clouds on the horizon that have nothing to do with the weather. Only Liz's daughter, who's found some of her mother's hidden journals, has any idea what's wrong. But by the end of the weekend, there will be no escaping the truth or its painful buried secrets. (Printed: $12.95; PDF eBook: $7.95; both together: $19.95, direct from publisher; eBook reader versions available at *www.Amazon.com*; *www.BN.com*; *www.eChristian.com*.)

Unless otherwise noted on the site itself, shipping is free for all products purchased through *www.healthylifepress.com*.

Life's A Symphony, by Mary Z. Smith – When Kate Spence Cooper receives the news that her husband, Jack, has been killed in the war, she and her young son Jeremy move back to Crawford Wood, Tennessee to be closer to family. Since Jack's death Kate feels that she's lost trust in everyone, including God. Will she ever find her way back to the only One whom she can always depend upon? And what about Kate's match making brother, Chance? The cheeky man has other ideas on how to bring happiness into his sister's life once more. (Printed book: $12.95; PDF eBook: $7.95; both together: $19.95, direct from publisher; eBook reader versions available at *www.Amazon.com*; *www.BN.com*; *www.eChristian.com*.)

From Orphan to Physician – The Winding Path, by Chun-Wai Chan, MD – From the foreword: "In this book, Dr. Chan describes how his family escaped to Hong Kong, how they survived in utter poverty, and how he went from being an orphan to graduating from Harvard Medical School and becoming a cardiologist.

The writing is fluent, easy to read and understand. The sequence of events is realistic, emotionally moving, spiritually touching, heart-warming, and thought provoking. The book illustrates . . . how one must have faith in order to walk through life's winding path." (Printed book: $14.95; PDF eBook: $8.95; both together: $22.95, direct from publisher; eBook reader versions available at *www.Amazon.com*; *www.BN.com*; *www.eChristian.com*.)

12 Parables, by Wayne Faust – Timeless Christian stories about doubt, fear, change, grief, and more. Using tight, entertaining prose, professional musician and comedy performer Wayne Faust manages to deal with difficult concepts in a simple, straightforward way. These are stories you can read aloud over and over—to your spouse, your family, or in a group setting. Packed with emotion and just enough mystery to keep you wondering, while providing lots of points to ponder and discuss when you're through, these stories relate the gospel in the tradition of the greatest speaker of parables the world has ever known, who appears in them often. (Printed book: $14.95; PDF eBook: $8.95; both together: $22.95, direct from publisher; eBook reader versions available at *www.Amazon.com*; *www.BN.com*; *www.eChristian.com*.)

The Answer is Always "Jesus," by Aram Haroutunian, who gave children's sermons for 15 years at a large church in Golden, Colorado— well over 500 in all. This book contains 74 of his most unforgettable presentations—due to the children's responses. Pastors, homeschoolers, parents who often lead family devotions, or other storytellers will find these stories, along with comments about props and how to prepare and present them, an invaluable asset in reconnecting with the simplest, most profound truths of Scripture, and then to envision how best to communicate these so even a child can understand them. (Printed book: $12.95; PDF eBook: $8.95; both together: $19.95, direct from publisher; eBook reader versions available at *www.Amazon.com*; *www.BN.com*; *www.eChristian.com*.)

Handbook of Faith, by Rev. Warren C. Biebel, Jr. – The New York Times World 2011 Almanac claimed that there are 2 billion, 200 thousand Christians in the world, with "Christians" being defined as "followers of Christ." The original 12 followers of Christ changed the world; indeed, they changed the history of the world. So this 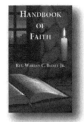 author, a pastor with over 60 years' experience, poses and answers this logical question: "If there are so many 'Christians' on this planet, why are they so relatively ineffective in serving the One they claim to follow?" Answer: Because, unlike Him, they do not know and trust the Scriptures, implicitly. This little volume will help you do that. (Printed book: $8.95; PDF eBook: $6.95; both together: $13.95, direct from publisher; eBook reader versions available at *www.Amazon.com*; *www.BN.com*; *www.eChristian.com*.)

Pieces of My Heart, by David L. Wood – Eighty-two lessons from normal everyday life. David's hope is that these stories will spark thoughts about God's constant involvement and intervention in our lives and stir a sense of how much He cares about every detail that is important to us. The piece missing represents his son, Daniel, who died in a fire shortly before his first birthday. (Printed book: $16.95; PDF eBook: $8.95; both together: $24.95, direct from publisher; eBook reader versions available at *www.Amazon.com*; *www.BN.com*; *www.eChristian.com*.)

How to Help a Heartbroken Friend, by David B. Biebel,

DMin – Helpful insights and guidelines for anyone who cares about those who are heartbroken and yet feels helpless in the face of the grieving. Learning to love quietly and share the burden as much as possible is a hard task, yet these thoughtful suggestions are bound to help one become an effective comforter. (Paperback: $10.00 at: www.healthylifepress.com.)

Dream House, by Justa Carpenter – Written by a New England builder of several hundred homes, the idea for this book came to him one day as he was driving that came to him one day as was driving from one job site to another. He pulled over and recorded it so he would remember it, and now you will remember it, too, if you

believe, as he does, that ". . . He who has begun a good work in you will complete it until the day of Jesus Christ." (Printed book: $8.95; PDF eBook: $6.95; both together: $13.95, direct from publisher; eBook reader versions available at *www.Amazon.com*; *www.BN.com*; *www.eChristian.com*.)

A HEALTHY LIFE PRESS BESTSELLER

A Simply Homemade Clean, by homesteader Lisa Barthuly – "Somewhere along the path, it seems we've lost our gumption, the desire to make things ourselves," says the author. "Gone are the days of 'do it yourself.' Really . . . why bother? There are a slew of retailers just waiting for us with anything and everything we could need; packaged up all pretty, with no thought or effort required. It is the manifestation of 'progress' . . . right?" I don't buy that!" Instead, Lisa describes how to make safe and effective cleansers for home, laundry, and body right in your own home. This saves money and avoids exposure to harmful chemicals often found in commercially produced cleansers. (Printed book: $12.99; PDF eBook: $6.95; both together: $16.95, direct from publisher; **full-color printed book: $16.99, only at** *www.healthylifepress.com*; eBook reader versions available at *www.Amazon.com*; *www.BN.com*; *www.eChristian.com*.)

TITLES RELEASED IN 2013

The Secret of Singing Springs, by Monte Swan – One Colorado family's treasure-hunting adventure along the trail of Jesse James. The Secret of Singing Springs is written to capture for children and their parents the spirit of the hunt—the hunt for treasure as in God's Truth, which is the objective of walking the Way of Wisdom that is described in Proverbs. (Printed book: $12.99; PDF eBook: $9.99; both together: $19.99, direct from publisher; eBook reader versions available at *www.Amazon.com*; *www.BN.com*; *www.eChristian.com*.)

God Loves You Circle, by Michelle Johnson – Daily inspiration for your deeper walk with Christ. This collection of short stories of Christian living will make you laugh, make you cry, but most of all make you contemplate—the meaning and value of walking with the Master moment-by-moment, day-by-day. (**Full-color printed book**: $17.95; full-color PDF eBook: $9.99; both together: $23.99, **only at *www.healthylifepress.com***; eBook reader versions available at *www.Amazon.com*; *www.BN.com*; *www.eChristian.com*.)

Our God Given Senses, by Gary A. Burlingame – Did you know humans have NINE senses? The Bible draws on these senses to reveal spiritual truth. We are to taste and see that the Lord is a good. We are to carry the fragrance of Christ. Our faith is produced upon hearing. Jesus asked Thomas to touch him. God created

us for a sensory experience and that is what you will find in this book. (Printed book: $12.99; PDF eBook: $9.99; both together: $19.99, direct from publisher; eBook reader versions available at *www.Amazon.com*; *www.BN.com*; *www.eChristian.com*.)

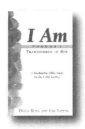

I AM – Transformed in Him (Volume 1) – by Diana Burg and Kim Tapfer, a meditative women's Bible study on the I AM statements of Christ in two 6-week volumes or one 12-week volume (12-week volume available 2014). Throughout this six week study you will begin to unearth the treasure trove of riches that are found within God's name, I AM WHO I AM. (Printed book: $12.99; PDF eBook: $9.99; both together: $19.99, direct from publisher; **COPIES OF VOLUME 1 AUTOGRAPHED BY BOTH AUTHORS ARE AVAILABLE FROM THE PUBLISHER, with free shipping: *www.healthylifepress.com*.** eBook reader versions available at *www.Amazon.com*; *www.BN.com*; *www.eChristian.com*.)

A HEALTHY LIFE PRESS BESTSELLER

Worth the Cost?, by Jack Tsai, MD – The author was happily on his way to obtaining the American Dream until he decided to take seriously Jesus' command to "Come, follow me." Join him as he explores the cost of medical education and Christian discipleship. Planning to serve God in your future vocation? Take care  that your desires do not get side-tracked by the false promises of this world. Learn what you should be doing now so when you are done with your training you will still want to serve God. (Printed book: $12.99, PDF eBook: $9.99; both together: $19.99, direct from publisher; eBook reader versions available at *www.Amazon.com*; *www.BN.com*; *www.eChristian.com*.)

 **VOWS**, a Romantic novel by F. F. Whitestone – When the police cruiser pulled up to the curb outside, Faith Framingham's heart skipped a beat, for she could see that Chuck, who should have been driving, was not in the vehicle. Chuck's partner, Sandy, stepped out slowly. Sandy's pursed lips and ashen face spoke volumes. Faith waited by the front door, her hands clasped tightly, to counter the fact that her mind was already reeling. "Love never fails." A compelling story. (Printed book: $12.99; PDF eBook: $9.99; both together, $19.99, direct from publisher; eBook reader versions available at *www.Amazon.com*; *www. BN.com*; *www.eChristian.com*.)

How to Obtain HEALTHY LIFE PRESS Resources

Our printed books are available from: *www.Amazon.com* and *www.healthylifepress.com*. Bookstores may order at a discount from the publisher. Inquire at: *info@healthylifepress.com*. Resources ordered directly through *www.healthylifepress.com* receive free shipping. Our e-Products are available from: *www.Amazon.com* (Kindle), *www.BN.com* (Nook), and for all commercial e-readers, through *www.eChristian.com*.

 **Nature: God's Second Book – An Essential Link to Restoring Your Personal Health and Wellness: Body, Mind, and Spirit**, by Elvy P. Rolle – An inspirational book that looks at nature across the seasons of nature and of life. It uses the biblical Emmaus Journey as an analogy for life's journey, and offers ideas for using nature appreciation and exploration to reduce life's stresses. The author shares her personal story of how she came to grips with this concept after three trips to the emergency room. (**Full-color printed book: $12.99, available direct from publisher with free shipping, or wherever books are sold**; PDF eBook $8.99; both together: $18.99, direct from publisher only; eBook reader versions available at *www.Amazon.com*; *www.BN.com*; *www.eChristian.com*.)

ABOUT HEALTHY LIFE PRESS

Healthy Life Press was founded with a primary goal of helping previously unpublished authors get their works to market, and to reissue worthy, previously published works that were no longer available.

Our mission is to help people toward optimal vitality by providing resources promoting physical, emotional, spiritual, and relational health as viewed from a Christian perspective. We see health as a verb, and achieving optimal health as a process—a crucial process for followers of Christ if we are to love the Lord with all our heart, soul, mind, AND strength, and our neighbors as ourselves—for as long as He leaves us here.

We are a collaborative and cooperative small Christian publisher. We work together; we share the proceeds fairly.

For information, e-mail:
info@healthylifepress.com.

RECOMMENDED RESOURCES – BOOKS

 **52 Ways to Feel Great Today**, by David B. Biebel, DMin, James E. Dill, MD, and Bobbie Dill, RN – Increase Your Vitality, Improve your Outlook. Simple, fun, inexpensive things you can do to increase your vitality and improve your outlook. Why live an "ordinary" life when you could be experiencing the extraordinary? Don't settle for good enough when "great" is such a short stretch further. Make today great! (Printed book: $14.99.)

New Light on Depression, a CBA Gold Medallion winner, by David B. Biebel, DMin, and Harold Koenig, MD – The most exhaustive Christian resource on a subject that is more common than we might wish. Hope for those with depression and help for those who love them. (Printed book: $15.00.)

 **Your Mind at Its Best – 40 Ways To Keep Your Brain Sharp**, by David B. Biebel, DMin; James E. Dill, MD; and, Bobbie Dill, RN – Everyone wants their mind to function at high levels throughout life. In 40 easy-to-understand chapters, readers will discover a wide variety of tips and tricks to keep their minds sharp. Synthesizing science and self-help, *Your Mind at Its Best* makes fascinating neurological discoveries understandable and immediately applicable to readers of any age. (Printed book: $13.99.)

The A to Z Guide to Healthier Living, by David B. Biebel, DMin; James E. Dill, MD, and Bobbie Dill, RN – Discover the top changes an individual can make in order to achieve optimal health. MSRP: $12.99; Sale: 8.99, while supplies last: *www.healthylifepress.com.*

RECOMMENDED RESOURCES
PRO-LIFE DVD SERIES

SEE *www.healthylifepress.com* (SELECT "DVD")

Window To the Womb (Pregnancy Care & Counseling Version) – Facts about fetal development, abortion complications, post-abortion syndrome, and healing. Separate chapters allow selection of specialized presentations to accommodate the needs and time constraints of each situation. (List Price: $34.95; Sale Price: $24.95.)

Window To The Womb (2 DVD Disc Set) Disc 1: Ian Donald (1910-1987) "A Prophetic Legacy;" Disc 2: "A Journey from Death To Life" (50 min) – Includes history of sonography and its increasing impact against

abortion—more than 80% of expectant parents who "see" their developing baby choose for life. Perfect for counseling and education in Pregnancy Centers, Christian schools, home-schools, and churches. (List: $49.95; Sale: $34.95.)

Eyewitness 2 (Public School Version) – This DVD has been used in many public schools. It is a fascinating journey through 38 weeks of pregnancy, showing developing babies via cutting edge digital ultrasound technology. Separate chapters allow viewing distinct segments individually. (List Price: $34.95; Sale Price: $24.95.)

COMBINATION Offer: Eyewitness 2 and Window to the Womb 2 (List Price: $84.90; Sale Price: $49.95.)

Made in the USA
Middletown, DE
20 August 2015